COALITION ARMOR VS IRAQI FORCES

Iraq 2003–2006

CHRIS McNAB

OSPREY PUBLISHING
Bloomsbury Publishing Plc
Kemp House, Chawley Park, Cumnor Hill, Oxford OX2 9PH, UK
29 Earlsfort Terrace, Dublin 2, Ireland
1385 Broadway, 5th Floor, New York, NY 10018, USA
E-mail: info@ospreypublishing.com
www.ospreypublishing.com

OSPREY is a trademark of Osprey Publishing Ltd

First published in Great Britain in 2024

A catalogue record for this book is available from the British Library.

ISBN: PB 9781472855749; eBook 9781472855732; ePDF 9781472855725;
XML 9781472855756

24 25 26 27 28 10 9 8 7 6 5 4 3 2 1

Maps by Bounford.com
Index by Fionbar Lyons
Typeset by PDQ Digital Media Solutions, Bungay, UK
Printed and bound in India by Replika Press Private Ltd.

Osprey Publishing supports the Woodland Trust, the UK's leading woodland
conservation charity.

A note on measure
Both Imperial and metric measurements have been used in this book. A
conversion table is provided below:
1in. = 2.54cm
1ft = 0.3m
1yd = 0.9m
1 mile = 1.6km
1lb = 0.45kg
1 long ton = 1.02 metric tonnes

1mm = 0.039in.
1cm= 0.39in.
1m = 1.09yd
1km = 0.62 miles
1kg = 2.2lb
1 metric tonne = 0.98 long tons

Author's acknowledgments
I would like to thank Nikolai Bogdanovic for his clear and considerate
editorial support throughout this project, and Adam Hook for his customarily
exceptional artwork.

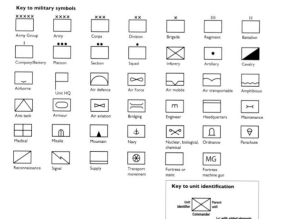

Front cover (above): A British Challenger 2 tank. (Adam Hook)
Front cover (below): An Iraqi T-72/Lion of Babylon tank. (Adam Hook)
Title page photograph: A Challenger 2 from A Squadron, Queen's Royal
Lancers patrols outside Basra, 2004. (Graeme Main/MOD/OGL v1.0)

CONTENTS

INTRODUCTION

On February 26, 1991, E Troop, 2d Squadron, US 2d Armored Cavalry Regiment (ACR) was advancing through southeastern Iraq. It was just one element amidst the massive Coalition army purposed with clearing Iraqi occupation forces from Kuwait in Operation *Desert Storm*. The 2d ACR was confronted principally by the mechanized and armored forces of the Iraqi Republican Guard (RG), regarded as Saddam Hussein's military elite, and the 50th Brigade of the 12th Armored Division. Most of the Iraqi crews were well armed and boasted many years of combat experience (the Iran–Iraq War had ended only three years previously). E Troop found itself in the vanguard of the offensive, its armored component consisting of nine M1A1 Abrams main battle tanks (MBTs) and 12 Bradley infantry fighting vehicles (IFVs). The only certainty in the desert ahead was that they would soon run into the enemy.

When E Troop made contact, it was in the form of a brigade from the RG *Tawakalna* Division. The Iraqis had pre-prepared a formidable defensive line of dug-in armor—including approximately 40 tanks and 16 BMP IFVs overlooking a ridgeline, heavily supported by emplaced infantry, armored personnel carriers (APCs), and with 18 more T-72s in reserve. On paper, the odds appeared impossibly stacked against the Americans.

Just after 1600 hours, the E Troop tanks ran into the Iraqi positions and the two sides began what became known as the Battle of 73 Easting, one of the largest armored engagements since World War II. Twenty-three minutes later, some 50 T-72s and more than 65 other Iraqi vehicles had been destroyed in a ferocious but truly one-sided battle. Across the wider battlefield of 73 Easting, the Iraqi forces lost more than 400 armored vehicles, while the United States suffered the destruction of one M2 Bradley, destroyed not by the Iraqis but by friendly fire.

The absolute dominance of Coalition armored forces was repeated throughout the short war. At the Battle of Norfolk on February 27, for example, just east of 73 Easting,

US and British forces annihilated approximately 850 Iraqi tanks and many other APCs and IFVs, for negligible comparative cost. By the time *Desert Storm* ended, 100 hours after it began, the Coalition had lost about 72 armored vehicles to all causes; Iraq's armored force had been depleted by an estimated 3,300 tanks and 2,100 IFVs/APCs.

Although many of the Iraqi armor losses were accounted for by Coalition air strikes, *Desert Storm* was still an unarguable demonstration of Western superiority in armored fighting vehicle (AFV) technology, tactics, and training. A letter written to *Armor* magazine for the July–August 1991 issue summed up the mood and the chief lesson:

> The resounding victory in the recent Gulf War validated to friend and foe alike the soundness of our Combined Arms Doctrine. More important, the necessity of heavy armor to that doctrine was clearly demonstrated. One might even go so far as to say that Armor was the keystone to the ground war victory.
>
> (Bashista 1991, p. 49)

Given that prior to the Gulf War some military analysts had been predicting the demise of heavy armor, for tankers there was evidently much to celebrate.

Over the next decade, the Western military world took a closer look at armored warfare doctrine, extracting the lessons learned and the necessary reforms to be made. As the Soviet Union finally collapsed, ostensibly removing the last major possibility of tank vs tank warfare, much of the focus turned to making armor lighter, more globally transportable and expeditious, the capabilities of vehicles defined by mobility, digital networking, and intelligent fire superiority. But it was also a time of real debate about the future of armor, an energetic confrontation of views. One particularly interesting voice was that of Lieutenant Colonel Ralph Peters, who on assignment to the Office of the Deputy Chief of Staff for Intelligence had responsibility for future warfare doctrine. In the fall of 1997, he published an article entitled "The Future of Armored

A US Marine Corps LAV-25 conducts training in October 2002, just months before Operation *Iraqi Freedom*. Both the 25mm gun and the gun's sights are gyro-stabilized, meaning that the weapon can be fired accurately on the move. During Operation *Iraqi Freedom*, the vehicles were fitted as standard with M240E1 machine guns on the turrets. (USMC)

Warfare" in the respected *Parameters* magazine. What was interesting about the article was not a bullish confidence about heavy armor on the open battlefield, but rather the creeping challenge faced by armor in urban warfare.

Traditionally, tanks have sought to avoid urban warfare. Deployed in narrow streets, the tank loses many of its advantages: crews have limited situational awareness; turret and gun traverse is restricted and elevation is often insufficient at close ranges; coordination between tanks and infantry units is problematic; the enemy can approach tanks from all directions unseen (including from above), easily deploying antitank weapons at close range on vulnerable parts of the vehicle (such as engine compartments); the environment is littered with objects and angles the armor crews must continually negotiate. Peters argued that urban combat, however, was a strategic certainty in the future landscape of warfare, stating: "Today's armor, designed for a war that—blessedly—never was, is ill-designed for urban combat. Yet, until better designs reach our soldiers, we will need to make do with what we have" (Peters 1997, p. 53).

Peters was absolutely prescient. On September 11, 2001, the United States came under unparalleled terrorist attacks, triggering the Coalition invasion of Afghanistan in 2001 and of Iraq in 2003. It was in Iraq that Coalition armor would fight Iraqi armor once again. But this would be a very different war to that of 1991. As we shall see, while there were some armored engagements over open terrain, much of the battle was drawn, as Peters predicted, into the towns and cities, where crews on both sides had to learn new rules of armored combat. Furthermore, the fall of Saddam Hussein's regime in April 2003 triggered a massive and persistent insurgency. Now the Coalition armor's greatest threat became the improvised explosive device (IED) and the rocket-propelled grenade (RPG), a form of fighting that inflicted armor losses far heavier than those experienced just over a decade previously.

This title seeks to give some shape to this story. It is a complex topic both technologically and tactically, with many vehicles and forces involved, so some compression is essential to make it digestible. Here our focus mainly rests upon a select few MBT and IFV types used by US, British, and Iraqi forces (without any intended disrespect for other Coalition partners) between the years 2003 and 2006. Within this spotlight, we study how the Iraq War provided the greatest tactical and doctrinal challenge to armored warfare since World War II.

A Warrior races across the arid scrubland outside Basra during Operation *Telic 1*. The vehicle is heavily laden with additional armor, which while appreciated for its extra protection could make vehicle handling more sluggish through the significant extra weight. (ESSAM AL-SUDANI/ AFP via Getty Images)

CHRONOLOGY

2003

March 20   Coalition forces launch the invasion of Iraq with Operation *Iraqi Freedom* (US) and Operation *Telic* (UK). I Marine Expeditionary Force (MEF) and the British 1st Armoured Division attack into southeast Iraq while the US V Corps drives north towards Baghdad.

March 21   Armored columns of 3d Infantry Division (3d ID) advance some 160km into Iraq and secure bridges over the lower Euphrates. UK forces secure the Al-Faw peninsula and close on Basra.

March 23–24   The 3d ID and USMC forces experience heavy fighting at Karbala and Nasiriyah respectively, on the route north to Baghdad. Eight Marine amphibious assault vehicles (AAVs) are destroyed in Nasiriyah on March 23.

March 25   3d ID battles the RG *Al-Medina* Division outside Karbala, inflicting major armor losses on the Iraqis.

March 27   British forces around Basra destroy numerous Iraqi armored vehicles attempting to advance out of the city. The Royal Scots Dragoon Guards (RSDG) begin Operation *Panzer* to aid beleaguered Royal Marines in southeastern Basra.

April 3   Battle of Mahmudiyah—US armor destroys multiple T-72s in a street battle in southern Baghdad.

April 5–9   3d ID pushes into Baghdad, resistance is overcome, and the regime of Saddam Hussein falls. By April 6, British forces have secured Basra.

May   In Baghdad, Fallujah, and Tikrit in particular, insurgency emerges and worsens, with mounting losses amongst Coalition forces. The insurgency spreads across the country.

June–December   Coalition forces begin conducting numerous detention and counterinsurgency operations, amidst rising guerrilla attacks.

2004

March–April   There is a dramatic intensification of the insurgency, particularly in Najaf, Kufa, Kut, Baghdad, Nasiriyah, Amarah, Fallujah, Ramadi, Baqubah, and Basra, with powerful insurgent groups seizing control of territory.

September–November   Coalition forces begin major operations to clear insurgent strongholds.

2005

November 2004–January 2005   US forces fight the Battle of Fallujah, one of the largest urban battles in post-World War II US history.

April–December   Following Iraqi elections, violence intensifies across the country. For US forces, Al-Anbar province (containing the cities of Fallujah and Ramadi) is the epicenter of the violence.

2006

Iraq descends into a state of civil war, with extreme levels of violence between opposing Iraqi militias and against Coalition forces.

DESIGN AND DEVELOPMENT

In some ways, the armored confrontations of Operation *Iraqi Freedom* (OIF) repeated patterns already seen in the preceding Gulf War. The Coalition operated MBTs and IFVs that had mostly entered development in the 1970s and 1980s specifically to meet the threat of the Soviet land army. The Iraqis, meanwhile, fielded a thick layer of ageing Soviet or Chinese armor with a thin cream of Western types on top.

But much had changed. Between 1991 and 2003, many of the Western vehicles underwent major upgrades, especially in the digitization of communications, navigation, and fire control systems (FCSs), but also with key hardware improvements, new variants, and the introduction of one new type (the Stryker). Iraq, by contrast, had much of its armor destroyed in more than a decade of conflict; the fleet that remained struggled to remain operational under the depredations of sanctions and time.

The sheer number of armored vehicles used by both sides in OIF makes it impractical to study each in depth in this volume. Here, therefore, we concentrate on principal MBT and IFV types, giving a brief insight into their origins and design concepts, but looking particularly at new models, upgrades, and significant field modifications made between 1991 and 2006.

MAIN BATTLE TANKS

UNITED STATES

The dominant US tank of OIF was the M1A1/A2 Abrams. Developed during the 1970s and 1980s, the M1 Abrams was purpose-designed to take on the new generations of Soviet armor (T-62, T-64, T-72). It offered a raft of innovations (admittedly not all convincing to the tank's critics): a multifuel-capable gas turbine engine; Chobham-type composite armor; computerized Future Combat Systems (FCS); nuclear, biological, chemical (NBC) protection; ammunition blow-out compartments. It originally had a 105mm Royal Ordnance L7 gun, but when it became clear that this was outclassed by Soviet tank firepower, it was replaced with a licensed Rheinmetall L/44 120mm smoothbore. The new gun resulted in the M1A1 variant, which entered production in 1984, and the IPM1 (Improved M1), which was an M1 with M1A1 enhancements applied. From May 1988 the M1A1 also received a first-generation depleted uranium (DU) armor layer to the turret to give extra protection against high-performance Soviet guns and ammunition—these tanks were called the M1A1 HA (Heavy Armor). Later versions fitted with 2nd-generation DU armor were labelled M1A1 HA+.

IPM1, M1A1, M1A1 HA tanks fought with distinction in the Gulf War. They were superb killers of enemy armor, but theater conditions also revealed their imperfections—they were very thirsty on fuel, mechanically sensitive, very heavy, and had some armor weak points. The period between 1991 and 2003, therefore, saw some significant upgrades.

A US military graphic of the M1A2 tank fitted with the Tank Urban Survival Kit (TUSK). Note the significant increase to the armored arrangements over the hull sides and the rear of the vehicle, plus the shielding provided for the loader and commander on top of the turret. The Remote Weapons Station (RWS) means the commander can fire his turret-mounted MG from inside the vehicle. (US DoD)

Remote weapons station

Loader's thermal sight

Thermal sight goggles

Loader's Armor Gun Shield

tank/infantry telephone

Rear protecting unit slat armor

Thermal sight components

Abrams Reactive Armore Tiles

In 1992, the next major variant went into production, the M1A2. This had transformational improvements in gun sighting (such as giving the tank commander his own independent thermal sight), improved FCS, updated navigation systems, and more computerized displays and controls. The improvements kept coming as the 1990s rolled on. From 1995 the M1A2 received the System Enhancement Package (SEP), which brought increased digitization to the vehicle's systems, including the introduction of the Force XXI Battle Command Brigade and Below (FBCB2) real-time networked communication platform, plus changes to the gunner's sight and to internal and radio comms.

The M1A1 was also being updated to keep pace with the M1A2. The M1A1 AIM (Abrams Integrated Management) substantially refurbished existing M1A1s to an almost as-new standard and also implemented upgrades to electronics, including the installation of the GPS-enabled Blue Force Tracking (BFT) system. During the 1990s all models of Abrams tanks began to benefit from the fitting of a diesel-powered External Auxiliary Power Unit (EAPU), at first fitted to the rear hull but later to the turret bustle. The EAPU allowed the tank to power important electronics without having to run the fuel-hungry turbine.

All such updates meant that the Abrams tanks of OIF were significantly more capable that those of *Desert Storm*. During OIF itself, towards the end of our period of focus, the most significant theater modification was the Tank Urban Survivability Kit (TUSK), announced in early 2005 and introduced progressively between 2005 and 2007. TUSK was an add-on armor kit designed to improve tank survivability in the new threat environment of Iraq, particularly the need to defeat RPG shaped charges. The TUSK I kit (there was a TUSK II kit introduced in 2008) featured Explosive Reactive Armor (ERA) tiles fitted to the side of the tank's hull; the individual

sections were officially known as XM-19 Abrams Reactive Armor Tile (ARAT). Not all tanks seen in Iraq, however, received a full TUSK modification; the application of the tiles could be varied according to unit and mission. The TUSK tanks were sometimes also fitted with dozer blades to remove street obstacles.

UNITED KINGDOM

The UK entered the Iraq War with what was effectively a new MBT, the FV4034 Challenger 2. The tank was a step-change evolution from its ancestor, the Gulf War workhorse that was the FV4030/4 Challenger 1. The Challenger 2 was developed by Vickers Defence Systems (sold to BAE Systems in 2004) as a 3rd-generation MBT during the second half of the 1980s, with the first tanks entering service in 1992. The Challenger 1 lent its successor elements of the hull and running gear, but ultimately the Challenger 2 was a ground-up redesign, with a new turret, enhanced armor and firepower, and modern digitized systems. Key changes included:

- A rifled 120mm L30A1 tank gun, with a modified breech and the ability to operate at higher pressures with updated ammunition types.
- A new L94A1 7.62mm chain gun (a version of the Hughes EX34), mounted coaxially to the upper left of the main gun.
- Protection provided by Dorchester Level 1 (DL1) armor, an upgrade of the famous but still secretive Chobham armor, with appliqué Operational Armour Packs (OAPs) taking the hull protection up to DL2, the side packs being Dorchester-grade inert panels while the front hull toe/glacis packs were ERA (Taylor 2018, p. 54).
- An improved CV12TCA engine with TN54 transmission.
- Enhanced FCS, giving greater automation of firing solutions and enhanced first-round hit.

This highly weathered M1A1 Abrams, seen here in Iraq in 2003, belonged to the US Marine Corps. The Marine M1A1s had the AN/VVS-2 passive night sight replaced with the Driver's Vision Enhancement (DVE), a superior thermal sight system. Marine tanks included other modifications to fire control and situational awareness. (US Navy photo by Photographer's Mate 1st Class Ted Banks)

A Challenger 2 of the Queen's Royal Lancers utilizes a General Support Bridge prepared by 2HQ Squadron, 32 Regiment, Royal Engineers, to cross an Iraqi defensive ditch at the beginning of the *Telic 1* invasion on March 21, 2003. The device projecting up in front of the commander's hatch on the turret is the Commander's Primary Sight (CPS), a panoramic day sight. (Cpl Paul (Jabba) Jarvis RLC/ MOD/OGL v1.0)

Further modifications were made to the Challenger 2 to meet its requirements for operations in Iraq (see artwork commentary). Furthermore, once Challenger 2s found themselves amidst a swelling insurgency in 2003, additional modifications had to be made in theater, to bring the tanks up to Theatre Entry Standard (TES). As with the US TUSK program, the British modifications were primarily focused on improving survivability in the face of IEDs, mines, and RPGs. Typical changes included the addition of under-belly and side appliqué armor, slat armor packs to defeat RPGs, and also electronic countermeasures (ECM) packages, specifically ECM antennae mounted on the fenders to detect/block IED signals.

A Challenger 2 patrols outside Basra, 2004. In total, 116 Challenger 2 tanks were deployed for the invasion of Iraq in 2003, separated into eight squadrons of vehicles and distributed between four major battlegroups. This vehicle belongs to A Squadron, Queen's Royal Lancers (QRL). (Graeme Main/MOD/OGL v1.0)

CHALLENGER 2, 7TH ARMOURED BRIGADE, BASRA, APRIL 2003

Crew:	4		Speed (road):	60km/h
Length hull:	8.3m		Speed (cross-country):	40km/h
Length overall (gun forward):	11.55m		Range:	450km or 550km using external tanks
Width:	3.55m including skirting plates		Armament:	1 × L30A1 120mm gun; 1 × 7.62mm L94A1 coaxial MG; 1 × 7.62mm L7A2 turret MG
Height:	3.04m			
Weight (combat):	64 tons			
Propulsion:	Perkins CV12 TCA 1200 Mo 3 Mk 6A generating 1,200bhp at 2,300rpm		Armor:	Dorchester-grade composite armor (depths confidential)

The Challenger 2 was one of the world's most capable MBTs, but OIF required further operational modifications to cope with both the hot and dusty conditions plus the specific threat environment. During the build-up to the invasion, the tanks received side and nose armor packs to enhance survivability. Combat Identification Panels (CIPs) and Thermal ID Panels (TIPs) were fitted to hulls and turrets (the slatted and white panels here seen fitted to the turret) to improve friend-or-foe identification by Coalition aircraft and other armor. Air filters were also upgraded to desert specifications. Tanks could be fitted with dozer blades to aid in driving through obstacles. This vehicle is based on a photograph of a Challenger 2 patrolling Basra in April 2003.

IRAQ

Iraq's MBT force in 2003 was a cluttered mix of several generations of Cold War imports, mostly of Soviet or Chinese origins but supplemented by smaller numbers of Western-sourced vehicles. The most obsolete of the bunch were T-54/55s, nearly 2,000 of which were purchased from Soviet/Eastern Bloc states between the late 1950s and mid-1980s. These were first-generation Cold War MBTs, with a low profile (about 30 percent less than Western tanks, a key characteristic of the Soviet tanks), 100mm D10-T rifled gun, and increasingly upgraded armor across the variants. The T-55 introduced a stabilized gun, NBC protection, infrared (IR) night vision, and improved ammunition storage. While the T-54/55s were respected when they first emerged, they were already heading towards obsolescence by the 1960s, and the numbers in Iraqi service by 2003 were low.

Iraq also bought more than 1,500 Type 59 and Type 69 tanks from China during the 1980s. The Type 59 was a Chinese version of the T-54A while the Type 69 was essentially a Type 59 but upgraded with features from the more advanced T-62 tank, which had entered Soviet service in 1961. An example of this tank had been captured by the Chinese during the Sino-Soviet border conflict of 1969, and the Chinese duly took what insights they could from the vehicle. These features included IR night-fighting capability, a laser rangefinder, and the V-12 diesel powerplant, but the Chinese also fitted a 100mm gun that could fire armor-piercing fin-stabilized discarding-sabot (APFSDS) rounds. In addition to the Type 69, Iraq also acquired 2,380 T-62s between 1973 and 1989. The T-62 is recognizably part of the family launched with the T-54/55, but it had a more powerful V-55 12-cylinder engine, thicker and more sloping armor, and, most crucially, a 115mm U-5TS (2A20) smoothbore gun with superior killing power.

An Iraqi T-55 sits forlornly in the desert on the outskirts of Basra in late March 2003, its crew having left it quickly. Such open terrain was lethal for Iraqi tanks, given that a Challenger 2 could outrange the Soviet-era tank by more than 500m and had better target acquisition and fire-control systems. (Spencer Platt/Getty Images)

TYPE 69-QM, IRAQI ARMY, 2003

Crew:	3	**Range:**	440km
Length hull:	6.24m	**Armament:**	1 × 100mm rifled main gun;
Length overall (gun forward):	8.58m		2 × 7.62mm coaxial and bow
Width:	3.31m including side skirts		MGs, 1 × 12.7mm antiaircraft
Height:	2.8m		MG
Weight (combat):	36.7 tons	**Armor:**	Steel, turret front 180mm
Propulsion:	12150L-7BW diesel		rolled homogenous armor
	developing 580bhp		(RHA)
Speed (road):	50km/h		

The Type 69-QM was essentially a Chinese Type 69-II exported and modified for Iraqi service during the 1980s. The Iraqi machine had a fully stabilized 100mm gun, a laser rangefinder, IR night vision, and a computerized FCS. Diesel could be sprayed over the hot exhaust to generate an improvised smokescreen. There were two Iraqi sub-variants: the QM1, which featured a 105mm rifled gun, and the QM2, upgraded to the Soviet 125mm smoothbore gun. Such conversions were probably limited in number.

US Marines inspect abandoned Iraqi T-72 tanks on April 12, 2003. The poor standards of maintenance in the Iraqi Army at this time are evident in these vehicles. Note, for example, the extensive corrosion around the fume extractor on the main gun and the crude application of side armor. (GYSGT Erik S. Hansen, US Marine Corps)

The most advanced tank in the Iraqi arsenal was the Soviet T-72, of which about 700 are estimated to have been in service on the eve of OIF, more specifically, the T-72M and T-72M1. Although these were export versions, they still offered the T-72's baseline advantages—a relatively lightweight, decent-mobility, low-profile, full-NBC-protected, and respectable armor (albeit thinner on the export models than on the Soviet ones). Its chief values, however, lay in its cheapness (hence the T-72 became the most widely distributed second-generation tank of the Cold War and beyond) and its powerful 125mm D-81/2A46 series main gun, with a 3,000–4,000m range for APFSDS and high-explosive antitank (HEAT) rounds and an auto-loading system that removed the need for a fourth crew member.

Countries rarely adopt export tanks without adaptations. Iraq was no exception, modifying all the imports cited above to meet local conditions. In terms of the T-55, Iraq produced several variant models in the 1980s and very early 1990s, although some were little more than minor experiments. The T-55QM, for example, was a T-55 fitted with a British Royal Ordnance 105mm L7 or the US 105mm M68, which married the L7's barrel and ammunition with a US-designed breech, mount, and recoil mechanism. The tank also featured a French-made laser rangefinder. The T-55QM2 had a longer 125mm cannon—L/52 instead of the 2A46's original L/48. (The "L" number is the length of the gun barrel in multiples of the caliber. The longer the barrel, typically the higher the velocity.) In 1989, according to some sources, a "T-72Z" was displayed at the International Arms Exhibition in Baghdad. This modified T-54, T-55, or Type 59 featured a 125mm gun with a repositioned fume extractor, an autoloader, a Slovenian EFCS-3 FCS, and a new transmission, plus the ability to take ERA panels. About 200 T-54/55s and 150 Type 59s are reputed to have been upgraded to the T-72Z standard, although the author has been unable to find more detailed confirmation. The T-55 "Enigma" upgrade, meanwhile, was a T-55 or Type 69 adapted to take spaced armor blocks designed to provide better protection against HEAT shells and antitank guided missiles (ATGMs).

In addition to the Enigma, the Type 69 emerged in several other Iraqi variants. The Type 69-QM (see artwork commentary) was a Type 69-II with a 100mm rifled gun, more extensive armor over the front plate, plus fittings for armor blocks, while the Type 69-QM1 had a 105mm NATO L7-type rifled gun and laser rangefinder. The Type 69-QM2, meanwhile, went for the power of a 125mm L/80 smoothbore gun and laser rangefinder.

Regarding the T-72, Iraq made various ongoing modifications to engine parts, shock absorbers, external fittings, and other relatively minor details, but the vehicle of note was the T-72 *Asad Babil* (Lion of Babylon), which was essentially a T-72M1 but indigenously built or assembled under license (see artwork commentary).

Alongside Soviet and Chinese armor, we should also note that Iraq acquired between 600 and 700 Western MBTs, either purchased direct or captured from Iran during the Iran–Iraq War. These types included US M48s and M60s, French AMX-30s, and British Centurions and Chieftains. But strict delineations of tank versions, upgrades, and modifications have to be taken with a pinch of salt by the days of OIF. Between the 1970s and early 2000s, Iraq's armored force had traveled a hard road, losing literally thousands of vehicles to war damage, age, a collapsing economy, and a degraded military infrastructure. Hidden in the official variants are endless improvisational modifications made simply to keep the fleet running. Certainly, the Western vehicles appear little in combat or in after-action photographs.

This T-72 *Asad Babil* (Lion of Babylon) tank was simply abandoned intact by its crew as Coalition forces approached in 2003. From this angle we can see the additional cast armor plating applied to the glacis. Also note the empty bracket on the right of the turret; sometimes this was seen fitted with an electro-optical countermeasures pod. (US Army)

ASAD BABIL, AL-MEDINA DIVISION, IRAQI REPUBLICAN GUARD, 2003

Crew:	4	Range:	425km, or 600km with
Length hull:	6.52m		external drums
Length overall (gun forward):	6.95m	Armament:	1 × 125mm 2A46M
Width:	3.59m		smoothbore gun; 1 × coaxial
Height:	2.23m		7.62mm PKT light machine
Weight (combat):	41.5 tons		gun; 1 × cupola mounted
Propulsion:	V-12 diesel generating 780hp		DShkM 12.7mm heavy
Speed (road):	60km/h		machine gun
Speed (cross-country):	45km/h	Armor:	45–300mm

The *Asad Babil* (Lion of Babylon) first rolled off Iraqi production lines in the spring of 1989 and it continued in manufacture during the 1990s. Theoretically, new features on the tank included laminated armor panels on the front and rear hull, thermal gunsights, reduced numbers of shock absorbers, and Chinese electro-optical dazzler active-protection systems, used to defeat incoming laserguided missiles. But overall, the *Asad Babil* was a poor-quality vehicle. The armor panels were of low-grade mild steel, many tanks were missing essential night-vision equipment (such as IR searchlights), and it even seems that the Iraqis were supplied with poorer ammunition, the APDS shells having an ineffective mild-steel core rather than tungsten. Fire-control electronics were also missing in many cases. Little wonder, therefore, that these tanks were mainly used as close-range defensive emplacements in 2003.

INFANTRY FIGHTING VEHICLES

UNITED STATES

The two chief US IFVs of OIF were the M2/M3 Bradley tracked vehicle and the LAV-25 wheeled vehicle. The picture is muddied by many other types of AFV fielded in the conflict, especially those of multi-vehicle families such as the Stryker, specialist armor like AAVs and the ever-creative proliferation of types based on the M113 APC. To keep our focus here, this study looks principally at the Bradley and LAV (Light Armored Vehicle), concentrating on US IFVs proper rather than carriers, but a general point is made about US vehicle modifications during the Iraq War.

During the Iraq invasion, but especially in the months that followed, it became apparent that most US vehicles in-theater required armor upgrades to survive IED and RPG threats. This problem was tackled with three levels of solution. Level I solutions were vehicles already designed to offer significant levels of armor protection. Deliveries of these were accelerating at the end of our period of study, in 2006. Before then, Level II and Level III solutions were implemented. Level II involved add-on armor kits, prefabricated in the United States, fitted to the vehicles to provide enhanced threat protection against IED blast/fragments, RPG strikes, and heavy direct automatic fire, while Level III consisted of improvisational steel plates found and added in-theater to give a better resistance to lighter fragments and assault rifle fire (Schulze 2006, p. 3). Add-on armor became a standard practice during OIF, on everything from High Mobility Multipurpose Wheeled Vehicles (HMMWVs—colloquial: Humvees) to Abrams tanks.

BRADLEY M2/M3

The Bradley IFV entered service in 1982 after a protracted, and controversial, development phase that began back in the 1960s. But the history of the Bradley

A Stryker lies on its side after being hit by an IED explosion while conducting operations just south of the Shiek Hamed village in Iraq in 2007, although both the crew and the vehicle would actually survive the blast. The IED had evidently been placed deep beneath the road surface. Note the heavy slat armor applied to the vehicle to protect against RPG strikes. (US Army, CC BY 2.0)

US soldiers from the 3d Armored Cavalry Regiment progressively mount into an M2A2 ODS Bradley during a combat patrol on the streets of Tal Afar, Iraq on February 6, 2006. From this angle we can see the thickness of the laminate armor panels fitted to the sides of the vehicle as additional protection against RPGs. (DoD photo by Staff Sgt. Aaron Allmon, US Air Force)

should not mask the excellence of the vehicle nor its tactical relevance to OIF. The Bradley provided toe-to-toe support to the Abrams MBTs and enhanced the firepower and mobility of mechanized infantry and cavalry operations.

There are two core versions of the Bradley: the M2 IFV, a mechanized infantry version with a three-man crew plus capacity for six fully equipped infantry; and the M3 cavalry fighting vehicle (CFV), a reconnaissance version with the three-man crew plus two scout troopers in the back. The baseline for both vehicles is a tracked and turreted IFV, sufficiently armored to protect the occupants against 14.5mm armor-piercing (AP) rounds and 155mm shell splinters, and armed with a 25mm M242 Bushmaster chain gun plus a coaxial 7.62mm M240C machine gun. From 1986, both the IFV and CFV were upgraded to the A1 variant, which introduced two Tube-Launched, Optically Tracked, Wire-Guided (TOW) ATGM missile launchers (one either side of the turret), an NBC system, plus various hull modifications (e.g. the M3A1 had its hull infantry firing ports removed in preference for periscopic vision).

Just prior to the 1991 Gulf War, the A2 models arrived. The Bradley now received a more powerful Cummins VTA-903T engine (the upgraded engine was necessary to handle the vehicle's increasing weight) and a significantly improved protective package that consisted of appliqué laminate armor, a kevlar spall liner, and attachment points for ERA tiles.

Desert Storm confirmed the Bradley's capabilities, but also highlighted issues only deployment and combat could reveal. The lessons learned fed into the Bradley Modernization Program (BMP), upgrading A1 Bradleys to A2 standard, A2s to an Operation *Desert Storm* (ODS) standard, plus the development of a new A3 variant. The ODS package improvements included:

- A redesigned rear troop compartment, with the mounted infantry facing inwards from seats along the sides of the hull (previously the seats were centrally placed, with the troops facing outwards).
- A GPS Tactical Navigation System (TNS).
- A laser rangefinder integrated with the GPS.
- Improvements to the Bushmaster barrel design.
- The FBCB2 system.
- A Driver's Vision Enhancer (DVE), enabling the driver to operate in complete darkness.

These modified Bradleys are known as the M2A2ODS and M3A2ODS.

The A3 variant came into service in the late 1990s, with a major revisioning of the vehicle's capabilities. The A3 was fitted with the new Improved Bradley Acquisition System (IBAS), which integrated all the vehicle's weapon optics and controls into digitized equipment that dramatically increased the range and speed of target acquisition and firepower, further enhanced by the addition of a second-generation forward-looking infrared (FLIR) system. The A3 commander also had a Commander's Independent Viewer (CIV) fitted on the turret, this being a FLIR/TV system that gave the commander 360° observation and target acquisition. All members of the crew, plus the infantry squad leader in the rear, had access to an FBCB2 system. The driver also enjoyed the navigation and DVE features of the ODS improvements.

The other major Bradley variant worth noting here is the M6 Bradley Linebacker Short Range Air Defense System, which is essentially an M2A2 but with its TOW launchers replaced by Stinger surface-to-air missile (SAM) pods. Although the M6 was purposely designed for air defense, the absence of air threats during OIF meant that the M6 was quickly repurposed for infantry fire support (Schulze 2006, p. 6). The M7 Bradley Fire Support Team Vehicle (BFiST), meanwhile, was also an M2A2 but with the TOW units replaced with target location sensors and fire-control systems, the vehicle acting as a hub for controlling artillery and air strikes.

As with other US vehicles, the Bradley received in-theater modifications during OIF. A 105-tile ERA kit was developed specifically for the Bradley, the tiles attaching via rails on the appliqué armor. At the end of our period of study, in 2006, the US Army also began developing a new Commander's Light Automatic Weapon (CLAW) equipment for the M2A3, which featured a 5.56mm M249 machine gun fitted to the CIV, for remote firing by the commander. The M2A2ODS, meanwhile, began to receive an additional machine gun on the turret in an M1 Loader's Weapon Mount, protected by an armored gun shield. Other Bradley improvements included a Power Line Protection (PLP) fitting to protect the vehicle from low-hanging power lines, a

This side view of a Bradley M2A3 conducting gunnery training stateside shows the extensive additional armor packages that the vehicle accrued based on the experience gained in Iraq. Many Iraq-deployed Bradleys had the Bradley Reactive Armor Tiles (BRAT) applied to the hull, rather than the passive laminate seen here. (Joseph H. Brown/US Army)

LAV-25, USMC 3D LIGHT RECONNAISSANCE BATTALION, FALLUJAH, 2004

Crew:	3 + 6	**Speed (road):**	100km/h
Length overall:	6.39m hull	**Range:**	668km
Width:	2.50m	**Armament:**	1 × 25mm M242 Bushmaster chain gun;
Height:	2.69m		2 × 7.62mm M240 MGs
Weight (combat):	16.14 tons	**Armor:**	Welded steel, 4.71–9.71mm
Propulsion:	Detroit Diesel 6V53T 300hp developing		
	275bhp at 2,800rpm		

The LAV-25 is the core IFV in the LAV family, an 8 × 8 wheeled vehicle carrying a three-man crew plus six fully equipped soldiers. The vehicle is fitted with a 25mm Bushmaster in a dedicated turret, plus has coaxial and turret-mounted 7.62mm M240 machine guns and eight smoke grenade dischargers. Power comes from a Detroit Diesel 6V53T turbocharged diesel engine, developing 275hp. The LAV-25's survivability is primarily dependent on its mobility, as its armor is light, and the vehicle is fully amphibious. Note that this vehicle also has a cowling fitted over the engine exhaust to reduce the thermal signature of the vehicle, a common practice in Iraq.

Combat Bumper to push through obstacles and walls, and a shorter-barreled M242 cannon to make traverse of the weapon easier in confined streets.

LAV-25

The LAV-25 emerged from a 1980s USMC requirement for a light armored reconnaissance vehicle. Following an evaluation of competitors, GM Diesel (General Motors of Canada) was selected for its license-built copy of the Swiss Mowag Piranha 8 × 8, part of the Armored Vehicle General Purpose (AVGP) or Light Armored Vehicle (LAV) family. The baseline model became known as LAV-25, and it entered US service in 1983.

Appliqué armor kits were developed for the LAV-25 during the 1990s. The most substantial of these packages came in 1998, with a Composite Ceramic Armor (CCA) kit that upgraded protection to 20mm armor-piercing (AP) rounds. From 2000, the LAV-25s in service went through the Service Life Extension Program (SLEP), with significant upgrades to electronics (including a driver's heads-up display), anti-corrosion treatments to the hull, and shrouds applied to the engine exhausts to reduce the vehicle's thermal signature. Combat experience in Iraq and Afghanistan led to a further SLEP program from 2004, which yielded a new variant, the LAV-25A2. Features of this upgrade included:

- A new appliqué armor suite to protect against IEDs, explosively formed penetrators (EFPs), and ammunition up to 14.5mm, with the addition of a commander's cupola shielded against small-arms ammunition. Survivability was also enhanced thanks to new fire-suppression equipment.
- Significantly improved optics, including a Raytheon Improved Thermal Sight System (ITSS) for both commander and gunner; the driver has an AN/VAS-5A(v)5 Passive IR sight system and three M-17 day periscopes.
- A gunner's eye-safe laser rangefinder for night operations, linked to an FCS modified to handle newer M919 APFSDS-T [Tracer] rounds.
- Improved communication systems, including the VIC-2 Intercom system and SINCGARS (Single Channel Ground and Airborne Radio System) RT-1523D VHR Radio.
- Significant reworking of the suspension and wheeltrain, necessitated by the additional weight of the other modifications.

It should be noted that the A2 variant officially did not enter service until 2007, but the application of A2 features to many A1 variants meant that some of the evolution of the A2 took place prior to the in-service date.

UNITED KINGDOM

WARRIOR

The FV510 Warrior family of tracked AFVs entered service with the British Army in 1985. In concept and practice, the Warrior essentially fulfilled the same roles in UK forces as the Bradley did in US forces, providing a fast, light, and potent vehicle for mechanized infantry and aggressive reconnaissance operations, capable of keeping pace with the heavy Challengers.

Development of the Warrior Mechanised Infantry Fighting Vehicle (MICV), to give its full name (although it was originally known as the MCV-80), was initiated to compete against new generations of Soviet IFVs. The MICV could take infantry into the heart of the battle with greater firepower, mobility, and survivability than earlier generations of British APCs. Like the other IFVs in this book, the Warrior was more of a family than an individual vehicle, but the core IFV was a tracked vehicle with a 3 + 7 crew, a Perkins CV-8 V-8 diesel engine, a turret-mounted 30mm RARDEN cannon, and a McDonnell Douglas EX-34 chain gun, designated in British service as the L94A1. Some vehicles were fitted with turret-mounted platforms for launching MILAN or, later, Javelin AT missiles.

Warriors served with distinction during the Gulf War, the experience resulting in in-theater modifications that included appliqué armor packages and the installation of GPS satnav systems. Most interesting to our story, however, are the upgrades and modifications made between 2001 and 2006. In 2001, Thales Group was awarded a £230 million contract to upgrade 455 Warriors and 146 Scimitars with thermal imaging sighting systems for the Battle Group Thermal Imaging (BGTI) program. This also included navigation equipment upgrades plus integration with the Bowman C4I communications system to improve combat communications between the Warriors and the Challengers. As Warriors encountered the same IED and RPG threats of other Coalition armor, they received additional protection in the form of the WRAP2 kit, composed of add-on passive armor and ERA panels plus bar armor to defeat RPGs. From 2004 some Warriors also received the Remote Controlled IED Electronic Counter Measure System (RCIED ECM), an electronic warfare

This FV107 Scimitar Light Tank from 1st Battalion, The Black Watch, is seen during a firepower demonstration on Salisbury Plain in 2005. Five years later, and partly in response to the experience in Iraq, the Scimitar Mk II emerged, with improved armor and blast resistance, better crew conditions, improved tracks and suspension, and an upgraded engine. (Graeme Main/ MOD/OGL v1.0)

(EW) suite designed to detect and jam enemy radio control signals used to detonate IEDs.

SCIMITAR

Another British AFV seen in OIF was the venerable FV107 Scimitar, the light reconnaissance vehicle amongst the Combat Vehicle, Reconnaissance, Tracked (CVR(T)) family that entered service during the 1970s. The Scimitar closely resembled its famous sibling the Scorpion light tank, another CVR(T) variant, although the Scimitar's defining armament was a non-stabilized 30mm L21 RARDEN cannon. Armor protection was light and resistant only to 12.7mm rounds. At only 7.8 tons in weight, the Scimitar was light, easily transportable, and fast, powered at first by a Jaguar J60 4.2-litre 6-cylinder petrol engine, then later by a diesel Cummins BTA 5.9 diesel.

Relatively small numbers of Scimitars were deployed during Operation *Telic* (the British element of the invasion of Iraq). Like the Warrior, the Scimitar received appliqué armor packages around the vehicle (including under-belly protection) and it was also the beneficiary of the BGTI program, the gunner and commander receiving thermal sights linked to the Bowman comms system.

IRAQ

At the beginning of OIF, Iraq's IFV force was a chaotic mish-mash of vehicles. As with MBTs, most of Iraq's IFVs had been sourced from Soviet, Eastern Bloc, and Chinese suppliers during the Cold War years. The armor fleet included prolific numbers of BTR-series APCs, BRDM-2 armored reconnaissance vehicles, plus smaller volumes of Czech OT-62 and OT-64 APCs, and other types. Some of these vehicles offered more

Seven Iraqi BMP-1 IFVs and an MT-LB-based armored ambulance (top left in the photograph) captured at Baghdad International Airport (BIAP), Iraq, during Operation *Iraqi Freedom*. The autoloader system on the BMP-1 meant that it had a cyclic rate of fire of 8–10rpm, although the weapon could also be loaded manually if need be. (Staff Sergeant Cherie A. Thurlby/USAF)

A severely damaged Iraqi BMP-2 lies alongside a road in northern Iraq in 2003. The side armor of the BMP-2 was only resistant to incoming projectiles up to 12.7mm (.50-cal) and therefore offered no protection against incoming Coalition IFV cannon fire; only the front armor was capable of resisting 25mm or 30mm rounds. (LCPL Andrew P. Roufs/USMC)

combat capability than mere infantry carrier types. Iraq's BTR-50P, for example, was fitted with 23mm ZU-23-2 antiaircraft (AA) cannon to create a self-propelled AA gun (SPAAG) platform, while the BTR-50PK replaced the 23mm firepower with twin 30mm M-53/59 autocannon in an open-tub mount. But the majority of the APCs were lightly armed with machine guns, and rarely intended to go into head-on engagements with other enemy armor.

Iraq's most powerful communist-sourced light armor was its fleet of BMP-1 and BMP-2 tracked IFVs. These had entered Soviet service in 1967 and 1980 respectively, but Iraq ordered extensive numbers from the Soviet Union and Czechoslovakia between 1973 and the late 1980s, with just under a thousand of both types remaining in service by 2003. Derived from the PT-76 light tank, the BMP-1 was a tracked and amphibious IFV with a 3 + 8 crew configuration. Its primary armament was a turret-mounted 73mm 2A28 Grom low-pressure smoothbore gun fed from an autoloader, but the vehicle also had a 9M14 *Malyutka* (NATO reporting name: AT-3 Sagger) manual command to line of sight (MCLOS) wire-guided anti-tank missile set above the gun barrel.

The BMP-2 was essentially an improved BMP-1, developed in light of BMP-1's combat experience gained during the 1973 Yom Kippur War. A key difference between the two types was that the BMP-2 had a larger turret that held both commander and gunner; only the gunner sat in the small BMP-1 turret. Turret armament for the BMP-2 was the 2A42 30mm autocannon and the 9P135M ATGM launcher capable of firing more modern types of semi-automatic command to line of sight (SACLOS)

ATGMs. The BMP-2 also reduced the number of troops carried to seven and its armor was marginally improved.

In addition to Cold War Soviet vehicles, Iraq also fielded limited numbers of European IFVs and light armored vehicles, sourced between 1968 and 1980. From France, for example, came the Panhard AML-60 and AML-90 armored cars, both 4 × 4 wheeled vehicles with light armor and turreted weapons. In the case of the AML-60, firepower was provided by twin 7.62mm machine guns and a breech-loaded 60mm mortar, while the AML-90 boasted a DEFA low-pressure 90mm rifled gun. According to the best available figures, Iraq acquired 131 AML-60s and 101 AML-90s between 1972 and 1980, but by the time of OIF possibly only 100–150 remained operational.

Looking beyond Europe, Iraq also supplemented its light armor with the Brazilian Engesa EE-9 Cascaval armored car, a 1970s 6 × 6 wheeled vehicle fitted with the turret of the AML vehicles. Like the AML-90, it also had a 90mm gun, the EC-90, a copy of a Belgian Mecar gun. Most of the c.400 vehicles purchased were lost in the Gulf War, but limited numbers of this type were present in 2003.

It is extremely difficult to discover how Iraqi IFVs were modified and upgraded between 1991 and 2003. The huge financial and trade embargo imposed by the United Nations Security Council (UNSC) on Iraq from 1990 severely degraded the Iraqi military during the rest of the decade, the Iraqi state largely being cut off from military imports and having a poor military manufacturing base. Spare parts for surviving armor ran low, often resulting in the cannibalization of vehicles. As we shall see, the armored force that faced the Coalition in 2003 was a shadow of that which faced it in 1991.

An Iraqi AML-90 light armored car captured in 1991 during Operation *Desert Storm*. The low-velocity DEFA D921 90mm rifled cannon was capable of taking shots out to 1,500m, but the vehicle had little chance against modern Coalition armor. Many AML-90s that survived until 2003 were destroyed by US Marines fighting around Nasiriyah. (Lance Cpl. Lanham/DoD)

THE RPG AND IED THREAT

Ultimately, the greatest threat to Coalition armor in Iraq came not from Iraqi tanks and IFVs, but from the chief antiarmor tools of the insurgency—the RPG and IEDs. Both were available to the insurgents in vast quantities, either through pre-invasion emplacement by loyalist paramilitaries or through the subsequent looting of military ordnance. (According to official sources, some 250,000 tons of ordnance went missing following the invasion.) The most prolific of the RPG types was the RPG-7, an unguided shoulder-launched weapon that fired shaped-charge HEAT, tandem charge, or HE/fragmentation warheads, with penetration of 250–750mm of RHA depending on the warhead type. The RPG-7 was a venerable type—it entered Soviet service back in 1961 and more than nine million units had been produced by 2004, making it the world's most widely distributed AT weapon. Iraq also had some more advanced RPG-29s in its arsenal. The RPG-29 entered Soviet service in 1989 and offered some significant advances over the RPG-7, including a greater effective range (450m vs 330m), improved sights, greater penetration via its 105mm PG-29V tandem-charge rocket, plus a "cold launch" facility—on firing, it did not generate the RPG-7's location-revealing backblast.

The RPG threat to Coalition armor was accompanied by the terrifyingly innovative and prolific use of IEDs. The design of these devices was limited effectively only by the imagination and available ordnance of the bomb cell, but they devolved down to three basic types: man-portable suicide bombs (essentially an insurgent wearing a bomb vest); static-emplaced IEDs; and vehicle-borne IEDs (VBIEDs). IED-detonating mechanisms became increasingly sophisticated over the course of the insurgency, starting with basic pull wires, timers, and mechanical detonators, but evolving into different types of remote detonation, such as using radio controls, cellphones, garage door clickers, and even IR lasers. Multiple IEDs (often mines, mortar bombs, or 155mm artillery shells) might be "daisy-chained" together with detonating cord to deliver a devastating area effect along the length of a convoy. IED emplacement was often ingenious. Any roadside object—a kerbstone, dead animal, pile of garbage, abandoned car, loose box, etc.—could hold an IED. By 2006 a new threat was emerging for armor, the explosively formed penetrator (EFP). The EFP was essentially a shaped charge that, when detonated, formed a hypersonic slug or jet that could penetrate armor from distance. Many of these were supplied by Iran, eager to aid the insurgency against the Coalition.

A member of the US 203d Military Intelligence Battalion inspects radio-control IED detonating systems found by soldiers of Company C, 1st Battalion, 327th Infantry Regiment, 1st Brigade Combat Team, 101st Airborne Division, near Hawijah, Iraq, in December 2005. (US Army photo by Spc. Timothy Kingston)

THE STRATEGIC SITUATION

The strategic objectives of OIF had a fundamental difference from those of the earlier Gulf War. This time, the Coalition was aiming at complete regime change. To begin nation building, therefore, the Coalition forces had to drive across the expanse of Iraq, secure major towns and cities (or at least ensure that they weren't a threat to the advance) on the way, converge on Baghdad, overthrow the government, and then quickly establish security and order in a leaderless and divided nation.

THE COALITION PLAN

The tactical plan for OIF was primarily based on a three-pronged drive from Kuwait across Iraq's southeastern border. (Initial planning envisaged a simultaneous surge from the north, but Turkey denied permission for the Coalition to use its country for land operations.) Armor would be at the vanguard of each combined-arms thrust.

The US elements of the invasion (forming the bulk of OIF) would undertake an offensive orientated roughly along the lines of the Euphrates and Tigris rivers, converging on Baghdad some 400km to the northwest. The US Army's V Corps was tasked with the westernmost push, its 3 ID following a path west of the Euphrates before crossing the river near Karbala and swinging northeast to make a "Thunder Run"

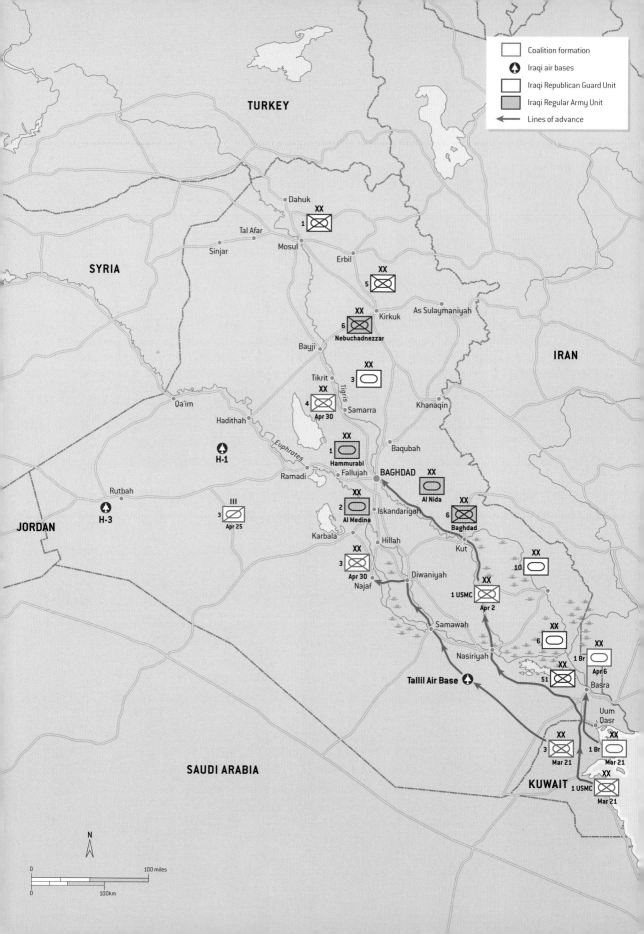

TURKEY

SYRIA

Dahuk

1 XX

Tal Afar

Sinjar

Mosul

Erbil

5 XX

Kirkuk

As Sulaymaniyah

6 XX
Nebuchadnezzar

Bayji

3 XX

Tikrit

Samarra

Khanaqin

IRAN

Qa'im

Hadithah

4 XX
Apr 30

Euphrates

1 XX
Hammurabi

Baqubah

H-1

Ramadi

Fallujah

BAGHDAD

Al Nida XX

Rutbah

III
3
Apr 25

JORDAN

H-3

2 XX
Al Medina

Iskandariyah

6 XX
Baghdad

Karbala

Hillah

Kut

3 XX
Apr 30

Najaf

Diwaniyah

10 XX

1 USMC XX
Apr 2

Samawah

6 XX

Nasiriyah

1 Br XX
Apr 6

Basra

Tallil Air Base

51 XX

Uum Qasr

3 XX
Mar 21

1 Br XX
Mar 21

SAUDI ARABIA

KUWAIT

1 USMC XX
Mar 21

N

0   100 miles
0   100km

Coalition formation

Iraqi air bases

Iraqi Republican Guard Unit

Iraqi Regular Army Unit

Lines of advance

into the capital. The 82d Airborne and 101st Airborne Divisions, meanwhile, would secure key urban objectives along the river, protecting the flank of the 3d ID advance. On the right flank of 3d ID, the 1st Marine Division, 1st MEF, would make a parallel advance, driving between the Euphrates and the Tigris before crossing the latter around Kut and then forming the right arm of the pincer that would close upon Baghdad. The 1st MEF would be supported by the 2d Marine Expeditionary Brigade (MEB), aka Task Force *Tarawa*, which had the initial task of seizing Jalibah Airfield in southern Iraq but subsequently became ensnared in the major battle to clear the city of Nasiriyah in the south. To the east of the Marines' start lines, the British 1st Armoured Division would perform Operation *Telic*, making a short right hook north and east to take the port of Umm Qasr, the Al-Faw peninsula, and Iraq's second city, Basra.

At the opening of the invasion, US Special Forces would make incursions into the west and north of Iraq to secure key airfields and towns. To provide some armor support in the north, TF 1-63 Armor of the 1st ID (the "Big Red One") was airlifted into Kurdish-controlled northern Iraq and attached to the 173d Airborne. (This was the first time that Abrams tanks had been air deployed for a combat operation.) The 4th ID—three brigades strong with similar levels of armor to the 3d ID—arrived north of Baghdad more than a month after the beginning of ground operations, their role being to secure the Samarra–Tikrit area, while the 1st Armored Division would follow on in May 2003 to take over security in Baghdad itself.

The bulk of the US armor (Abrams and Bradleys) in V Corps was contained in the 3d ID's armor and mechanized battalions. The division was split into three Brigade

OPPOSITE: Coalition operations, Iraq, March–April 2003.

USMC LAV-25s are readied for deployment in December 2003. These particular vehicles are assigned to the 13th Marine Expeditionary Unit (13th MEU), 1st Light Armor Reconnaissance Battalion Landing Team (1st LAR BLT 1/1). The M242 cannon of these vehicles are nearing or at the vehicle's maximum gun elevation of +60°. (US Navy photo by Photographer's Mate 1st Class Ted Banks)

Combat Teams (BCTs), sub-divided into three or four battalion-sized armor or mechanized infantry task forces plus an artillery battalion. The 1st and 3d BCTs both had two mechanized infantry battalions and an armor battalion, while the 2d BCT had two armor battalions, one mechanized infantry battalion, and the 3d Sqn, 7th Cavalry Regiment. The 2d Brigade, 101st Airborne, also had the 2d Battalion, 70th Armor Regiment (2-70 Armor) attached in support, giving the light airborne troops the support of Abrams muscle.

In total, the US forces that began OIF wielded a total of about 850 MBTs in-theater; naturally, fewer were deployed at the tip of the combat spear. A USCENTCOM (United States Central Command) source stated that on March 17 the 3d ID had 200 M1A1s and 200 M2 Bradleys ready to roll, while press sources indicated that the 1st MarDiv had 150 M1A1 tanks (Cordesman 2003, p. 42).

Looking at the British contribution, the 1st (UK) Armoured Division brought to the fight approximately 116 Challenger 2s, 140 Warriors, and 66 Scimitars, plus substantial numbers of specialist armored vehicles. The heavy armor was operated by the Royal Scots Dragoon Guards (RSDG) and the 2nd Royal Tank Regiment (RTR), working in cooperation with two mechanized infantry battalions: the 1st Battalion, the Black Watch, and the 1st Battalion, Royal Regiment of Fusiliers. The 3rd Regiment Royal Horse Artillery provided self-propelled artillery support.

IRAQI FORCES

It is difficult to ascertain with precision the strength of Iraqi forces in March 2003. The Iraqi Army had been malformed by years of war, mismanagement, austerity, and corruption, with divisions typically running at 50–75 percent reduced strength. Nevertheless, the Coalition war planners were both respectful and nervous about what remained one of the largest land armies in the world, with a manpower of *c.*400,000 active-service troops plus a reserve pool of 650,000 men and no governmental qualms about conscripting hundreds of thousands more personnel. Saddam's regime could also draw upon *c.*100,000 paramilitaries, the bulk composed of police and security forces, plus 30,000–40,000 *Fedayeen Saddam* (Saddam's Men of Sacrifice), regime loyalists with much fanatical enthusiasm and some military training. Saddam had also made plans (building on earlier moves in the 1980s) to foster a multi-million warrior militia, the Popular Army, embedded within the citizenry and ready to transform Iraq's urban areas into fortress breakwaters for invaders. Although this never materialized in actuality, some of the asymmetric infrastructure (arms caches, anti-tank ditches, etc.) were encountered in pockets of resistance by the Coalition troops.

On paper, Iraq's armor force was much diminished from its heyday but was still formidable, having somewhere between 2,200 and 2,600 MBTs. Only 1,800–2,000 were combat capable, however (Cordesman 2003, p. 47). In terms of IFVs, the Iraqis had the mixed bag of vehicles described previously. The largest portion of the IFV fleet were the BMP-1/2s, of which the Iraqis had about 1,200, but there were at least another 1,500 pieces of infantry armor available, if we include APCs.

At the time of the invasion in March 2003, Iraqi armor was divided between the regular army and the Republican Guard (RG). There were six RG divisions in total, and three of those were armored and one mechanized, while the army had three armored and three mechanized divisions. As a general rule, the Republican Guard received the superior equipment, therefore many of the T-72s were in their hands. It is difficult to say how many tanks would have been in each division, but Cordesman lists RG armored divisions as operating 175–300 tanks, while regular army divisions had 175–200 (Cordesman 2003, p. 45). The RG likely operated about 750 T-72 and *Asad Babil* tanks.

In terms of the deployment of Iraqi forces, the army divisions largely hugged the eastern areas of the country, running the full length of the border with Iran and into the northern Kurdish zones. The heaviest concentrations of divisions were in the northeast and southeast, the central portion of Iraq being more the province of the ever-faithful RG. Regular army armored units in the immediate line of Coalition advance in the south (the province of the army's III and IV Corps) included the 6th and 10th Armored Divisions and the 51st Mechanized Division.

The RG, with a strength of 60,000–70,000 men, was separated into two corps: Northern/I Corps and Southern/II Corps. It included the Iraqi military's most potent armored formations: the *Al Nida*, 2d *Al-Medina*, and 1st *Hammurabi* armored divisions and the 5th *Baghdad* and 6th *Nebuchadnezzar* mechanized divisions. The armored divisions and several of the mechanized divisions formed a protective ring around Baghdad. In addition, Saddam's Special Republican Guard (SRG)—a personal

Although most of Iraq's ZSU-23-4 self-propelled 23mm antiaircraft guns were destroyed in 1991 (this specimen was simply abandoned at that time), small numbers remained to engage Coalition vehicles in 2003. The stream of 23mm shells, typically a mix of fragmentation and armor-piercing rounds, posed a serious threat even to heavy Coalition armor. (US DoD)

security force that had little interaction with other military forces—also had possibly as many as 100 T-72 tanks in its tables of organization and equipment (TO&E).

In the spring of 2003 Iraq had a relatively coherent on-paper regional command structure, but in reality the country's armed forces were in no way ready to defend against what was massing against them. There were opportunities, however, to disrupt and delay a superior force. The two main threats to the Coalition at the start of OIF were the long, exposed flanks they would create as they pushed ever farther north and, more worryingly, the Iraqis turning towns and cities into densely defended fortresses, drawing Coalition troops into attritional urban combat that leveled out imbalanced force ratios. As we will see, the first of the threats never materialized but the second was implemented vigorously, especially during the insurgency. Iraq certainly had the means to make the Coalition advance slow and costly. What it did not have was the innovation and decentralized decision-making that characterizes a modern professional army (to be discussed below). Nor did it have the sophisticated command-and-control, intelligence, surveillance, target acquisition, and reconnaissance infrastructure and expertise. As such, the Iraqi Army was destined for defeat.

TECHNICAL
SPECIFICATIONS

As this book deals with multiple types of AFV, running through the detailed technical specifications of each would become a rather tedious exercise in bare data presentation, missing some of the key contexts for understanding the armor in terms of combat capability. In this section, therefore, we will descriptively compare some select adversarial pairings. Through this approach, we can note the relative strengths and weaknesses of key types in relation to the three classic parameters informing armor design: mobility, firepower, and survivability. The pairings are chosen to enable the reader to extrapolate to other vehicles.

This grainy image shows a collection of metal disks intended for use in explosively formed penetrators (EFPs). The device would concentrate explosives behind the disk (i.e. pressing against the convex face). When the explosives were detonated, the disk would collapse into a hypersonic metal slug that could penetrate heavy armor. (US DoD)

T-72M VS M1A2 ABRAMS

The T-72M and the M1A2 Abrams represent the pinnacle of the two opposing armor forces at the beginning of OIF. As we shall see, this was not a contest of equals.

The overall dimensions and weights of the two tanks are quite different. The T-72M, for example, had a hull length of 6.95m, a width of 3.59m, and height of 2.22m, with an overall weight of 46 tons. The M1A2 SEP, by contrast, had a hull length of 7.93m, width of 3.66m, height of 2.44m, and, most notably, an all-in

weight of 65 tons. The T-72 tank, therefore, was both smaller and lighter than its US counterpart, and boasted a key advantage in its low silhouette. Being tighter to the ground made the T-72 harder to spot and hit, especially when behind cover, plus more difficult for enemy combatants to identify its type and threat level. All these factors theoretically increased the tank's chances of survival in combat situations, if the crew handled the tank well, of course (a big "if," as we shall see).

The T-72's compact dimensions were partly the result of the decision to install an auto-loader mechanism in place of a human loader. The upshot, however, was that the interior of the T-72 was quite cramped, with much of the space taken up by the auto-loader cassette and gun breech. When the hatches were closed, the commander and gunner could not stand freely, a physical limitation that took a toll on the three-man crew's psychology and performance during extended operations. In contrast, the M1A2, while not exactly spacious, provided a more comfortable environment for its four-man crew.

When it came to mobility, the M1A2 Abrams and T-72 tanks passed the baton of advantage between them. The M1A2 was marginally faster on the roads, reaching speeds of up to 67km/h compared to the T-72's maximum speed of 65km/h, but the T-72 had a longer operational radius, with a range of 550km on roads when fitted with long-range fuel tanks, compared to just 426km for the M1A2 on the road, despite the US tank carrying more fuel. (The Abrams was a thirsty beast—it did about 0.6mpg.) The M1A2 did have an advantage in vertical obstacle clearance, being able to surmount obstacles up to 1.24m high, while the T-72 could only handle obstacles up to 0.85m high. However, the T-72 had a slight edge in trench crossing, with a maximum width of 2.8m compared to 2.74m for the M1A2.

Both tanks were well-armed, but taking into account all the factors affecting gunnery, the two tanks were not equal in terms of firepower and lethality. The T-72's 2A46 (D-81TM) cannon had an effective range of 3,000–4,000m for APFSDS,

HEAT, and HE-Frag rounds, and could reach even longer ranges when firing ATGMs (up to 9,000m), although the firing of missiles from the gun tubes was not a common practice for Iraqi T-72 crews, if indeed it was done at all. The T-72's armor penetration capability was, nevertheless, a concern for crews of Coalition AFVs, the 2A46 offering typical APFSDS penetration of 245–495mm at 0° and 140–250mm at 60°, and HEAT rounds being able to penetrate up to 300mm at 60°. The T-72 also had a fast rate of fire, its auto-loader capable of 8rpm, and its gun stabilized both horizontally and vertically for firing on the move.

The T-72's fire control system, however, was technologically primitive compared to that of the Abrams, relying more on manual input of data into an analog ballistic computer, without automatic corrections for factors such as barrel wear and weather conditions. This meant that firing on the move was possible only at slow speeds, with long-range shots best attempted when the T-72 was brought to a complete stop. The Iraqi T-72 also lacked the sophisticated night-fighting system of the Abrams. The T-72M tank was equipped with a passive image-intensification night-vision system that allowed the gunner to operate in low-light conditions, with an active IR "Luna" searchlight providing an artificial light source in conditions of complete darkness. The commander had his own small IR searchlight separate from the Luna searchlight, plus a binocular-type image-intensification sight for use outside the tank. By 2003 (indeed by 1991), this arrangement was far from satisfactory, as its capabilities were well beneath those of modern NATO thermal night-fighting sights, which worked by detecting heat signatures and gave more effective targeting in low-light conditions.

An abandoned Iraqi T-55 in Ramadi, August 2003, becomes the focal point for local sheep grazing. It has been stripped of its turret-mounted MG and infrared searchlight. The armor crew likely deliberately positioned themselves amongst the palm trees as cover, although this position evidently was not conducive to turret traverse. (KARIM SAHIB/AFP via Getty Images)

The M1A2 Abrams (and many of the upgraded M1A1 variants), by contrast, offered cutting-edge fire control that, when married with excellent standards of crew training, constructed a superior battlefield package during OIF. The 120mm M256 gun itself had a maximum effective range of 3–4km, reaching up to 5km for SEP variants with the most advanced fire-control packages. Automation was the heart of the Abrams FCS. The ballistic solution was derived partly from crew-provided information and a laser rangefinder, but was heavily refined by data delivered from multiple sensors automatically inputting factors such as crosswind, air temperature and humidity, barometric pressure, the cant and roll of the vehicle, ammunition type, barrel drop, barrel condition, ammunition temperature, and target speed and direction, the fire-control computer updating all such information at a rate of 30 times a second to produce a 95 percent first-round-hit probability. All the commander or gunner had to do was to keep the reticle affixed on the target. The CITV system also allowed the commander to acquire targets across a 360° spectrum even as the gunner was engaging other targets, producing faster follow-up shots and enhancing situational awareness.

The Abrams' commander and gunner were able to select from two potent APFSDS ammunition types—the M829A1 and the improved M898A2, giving penetration through c.700mm and 740mm of RHA respectively. Other ammo choices were the M830, the standard HEAT round capable of penetrating 600mm RHA, and the M830A1 MPAT (Multipurpose Anti-Tank), which delivered a similar penetration to the M830A1 but also had good utility as a bunker-busting round and was fitted with a proximity fuse useful for engaging moving air and ground targets and for delivering air burst. Theoretically, the T-72's autoloader gave the Soviet-era tank an advantage in terms of speed reloading, but a well-trained Abrams loader could match the 8rpm rate of fire through muscle-power alone, albeit only for short periods (4rpm was a more comfortable rate).

Although the T-72 was capable of significant armor upgrades through add-on passive and ERA tiles, the Iraqi T-72s seen in photographs from 2003 are largely without such packages, with the exception of occasional steel-reinforced rubber skirting to protect the tracks. In their bare format, the Iraqi T-72s were therefore profoundly vulnerable to Abrams shells. T-72 armor varied between cast, RHA, and laminated sections, varying in depth between 80mm on the lower nose and the hull up to 335mm on the turret cheeks. Taking into account the angle of the armor, the T-72 has been calculated as offering protection equal to 280–380mm RHA against APFSDS and 490mm RHA against HEAT; the glacis provided 400mm against APFSDS and 490mm against HEAT. Comparing these figures with the Abrams' penetration data above, the basic message is clear—the T-72 was unlikely to survive a hit from the Abrams' main gun, a theory borne out in reality.

The Abrams, conversely, had truly muscular armor protection, as we would expect for a vehicle of its weight and size. The frontal turret armor on an M1A2 SEP has been estimated to give protection equivalent to up to 960mm against APFSDS and 1,300mm for HEAT, with the glacis giving 590mm and 1,050mm respectively against the same shell types. Protection is significantly lower on the upper glacis (thinly armored because of its near-horizontal profile, hull sides, and rear of the vehicle), but overall the Abrams was well-placed to defeat T-72 rounds, especially once enhanced with add-on features such as slat armor, armor laminate, and ERA.

The Abrams' survivability was enhanced by further core design features. It included, for example, blow-off compartments for main ammo storage in the hull and turret. If the ammunition store was hit or cooked off, the compartment panel would blow out and the fire/explosion would be vented away from the crew compartment, also reducing the risk of a catastrophic explosion. The T-72 had no such feature. Indeed, the ammunition storage necessitated by the auto-loader actually made the tank more vulnerable to major explosions, which explains why we see so many images of killed T-72s with their turrets lying at a distance from the charred hull.

BRADLEY M2A3 VS BMP-2

The peer competitor for the Bradley M2A3 in OIF was the Iraqi BMP-2. The Bradley's basic dimensions come in at 6.55m long, 3.28m wide (without an armor kit), and 2.97m high to the top of the turret roof. Total combat weight was 29 tons, or 32.7 tons with add-on armor. The BMP-2's dimensions reflected the low-profile, lightweight philosophy of Soviet armor design—6.74m long, 3.15m wide, and 2.25m high, the vehicle weighing a total of 14.3 tons, substantially below the mass of the Bradley.

The M2A3, however, had a far more powerful engine, producing about double the horsepower of the BMP-2. Consequently, the two vehicles locked horns reasonably equally over performance. The Bradley's top road speed was 56km/h, the BMP-2's 65km/h. In terms of gradient and side slope traversing, both vehicles operated at maximums of 60 percent and 30 percent respectively. The Bradley had a slight edge in climbing vertical obstacles—0.8m as opposed to the BMP-2's 0.7m—but the BMP-2 had better trench crossing, 2.5m vs 2.1m. As with the T-72 over the Abrams,

Bradley M2 vehicles are seen here conducting an exercise in the 1990s. Although the Bradley had a somewhat difficult birth and development phase, it has proved to be one of the most effective pieces of armor in the modern US military, a highly workable blend of firepower, mobility, and protection. (US Gov)

the BMP-2 had a much better fuel economy and therefore operational radius: 600km on the road compared to 400km for the Bradley.

A firepower comparison shows the two vehicles roughly evenly matched in terms of basic hardware and fundamental ballistics. The BMP-2's main armament was a two-axis stabilized 30mm 2A42, sending out armor-piercing rounds to an effective range of 2,000m and HE rounds to 4,000m. The stabilization meant it could fire accurately on the move, while 360° turret traverse facilitated all-round defensive response. The gun could be fired in three modes: single shot; 200–300rpm auto; 500rpm auto. A coaxial 7.62mm PKT machine gun provided suppressive fire against light targets and personnel. The vehicle also had a turret mount for a single AT-4 Spigot or AT-5 Spandrel ATGM, ranged out to 4,000m.

Set side-by-side with the 2A42, the Bradley's Bushmaster actually had inferior performance. The effective range of the 25mm round was approximately 1,500m for AP rounds and 2,000m for HE rounds. Plus, the Bradley had far fewer rounds on board: the BMP-2 carried 2,000 rounds of main gun ammunitions, while the Bradley had just 900. The Bradley did, however, carry TOW missiles (two pre-loaded in the units, two as reloads), which had a roughly comparable range to the Spandrel of 3,750m.

So, the Bradley and the BMP-2 could go roughly toe-to-toe in a missile and gun fight. But as with the Abrams, advanced technology tipped the balance in favor of the Bradley. The M2A3's digital FCS was far more capable than that of the BMP-3, with faster target acquisition, better night-fighting systems, and excellent networked situational awareness, all things lacking on the ageing Iraqi BMP-2s. The US Bradleys also enjoyed better armor protection in OIF. The M2A3's mix of welded aluminum and spaced laminate armor was supplemented in-theater by passive and ERA add-on armor, giving it excellent protection against the BMP-2's 30mm rounds as well as RPGs and ATGMs. The naked Iraqi BMP-2s had protection against 23mm AP rounds fired at 500m and 7.62mm AP at 75m, but it was quite vulnerable otherwise.

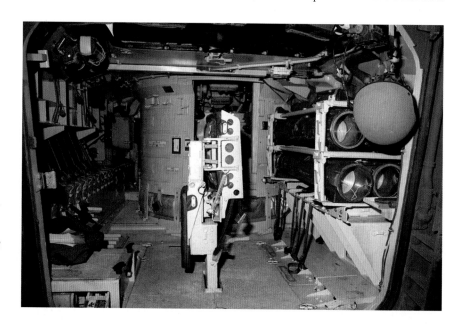

The rear crew compartment of a Bradley M3, showing the seating for the three reconnaissance scouts. The tubes to the right of the vehicle are for additional TOW missiles. The M3 did away with the hull firing ports fitted on the early M2 models. (SPC Diana Lindsey/US Army)

M242 25MM CHAIN GUN IN M2A2 BRADLEY TURRET

The Bradley's turret was dominated by the M242 Bushmaster 25mm gun (**1**). The weapon was a chain-gun type, powered by a single 1.5hp DC motor or newer 1.0hp motors. A dual-feed system allowed it to feed either AP or HE cartridges, with one ammunition box holding 70 rounds and the other box 230 rounds (each box could feed either AP or HE). The gunner (**2**) or commander (**3**, both could operate the weapon) had the choice of three rates of fire: single shot; low rate (100rpm +/−25rpm); high rate (200rpm +/−25rpm). In addition to traditional visual methods of range estimation, the gunner could use the AN/GVS-5 laser rangefinder to determine firing distance with more precision, and both commander and gunner had access to the Eye-Safe Laser Range Finder (ELRF, **4**), which displayed range in 5m increments from 190m to 9,990m. The field manual FM 3-22.1 (FM 23-1) *Bradley Gunnery* notes "The BC [Bradley commander] might have to lay the gun for direction if the gunner's scan is far from the target. The BC releases control to the gunner (target handoff) and issues the fire command" (Department of the Army 2003, 6.29). If engaging an armored point target (such as an enemy IFV), the gunner would typically lay down fire in 3–5-round bursts, observing impacts and effects until the target was suppressed. The Bradley's secondary armament comprised the M240C machine gun (**5**).

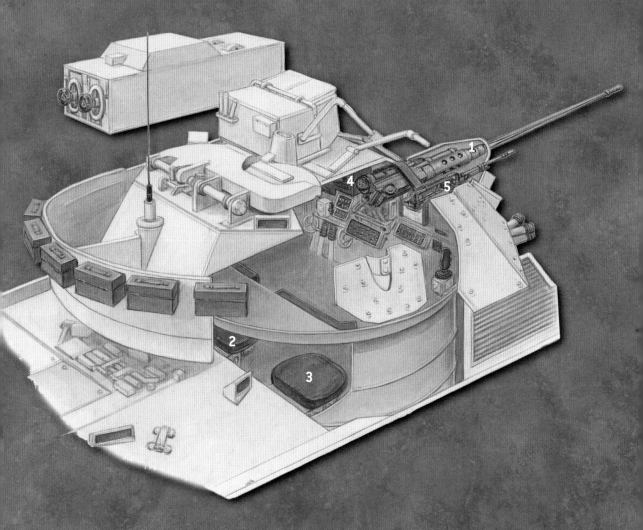

RPG/IED VS WARRIOR

The battle between the Warrior and RPGs/IEDs in Iraq cannot be reduced to a simple contest between warhead and armor. RPGs, for example, obviously required users to operate them. In most cases, in urban environments those users were firing from ranges of under 100m thus, if spotted, they could be targeted and engaged by the Warrior's heavy firepower, ideally before the insurgents had time to attack. Furthermore, the Warrior's seven mounted infantry were also part of its defensive package—the infantry could be deployed to engage the insurgents and protect the vehicle.

The Warrior's 30mm RARDEN cannon had an effective range of about 1,500m for AP rounds, and a maximum range of 3,000m when firing HE rounds. Mixed types in the ammunition feed were standard in Iraq, giving the Warrior gunner penetration through hardened armor via the AP and area destruction via the HE. The problem with the RARDEN, however, was that it was loaded from three-round clips rather than from a belt, slowing the overall rate of fire. Also, the gun was not stabilized on any plane; it could be fired on the move, but its accuracy was severely compromised in this mode. (After our period of study, the Warrior received investment towards a fully stabilized gun.) The 7.62mm Hughes chain gun (the Warrior's secondary armament), was also prone to stoppages because of its vertical feed from below, fighting against the pull of gravity.

The Warrior's chief strength in terms of survivability was its speed. It could sprint along at 74km/h, much faster than the Bradley. Plus, it had respectable welded aluminum Chobham-type armor, securing the crew not only against 155mm shell

The crew of a Warrior armored vehicle engage in discussion with unsettled locals south of Basra on March 27, 2003. Note that this vehicle has a turret-mounted MILAN ATGM launcher, a wire-guided semi-automatic command to line of sight (SACLOS) missile with a range of about 2,000m. Later the Warriors were fitted with more advanced Javelin systems. (Spencer Platt/Getty Images)

splinters and 14.5mm rounds but also (as we shall see below) against many RPG warheads, especially when bolstered by appliqué armor tiles and Enhanced Protection Bar Armour (EPBA). The Thales/Optronics Battlegroup Thermal Imaging (BGTI) system that came into service in 2004 also gave the gunner 8× zoom vision at night, plus fast communications with other vehicles in the battlegroup.

So the Warrior was a hard nut to crack, but this did not mean that it was invulnerable. Multiple hits from RPGs could and did destroy Warriors in Iraq. IEDs were also a prevalent threat. As the conflict showed, even the heaviest MBT could be destroyed by an IED if the device was large enough. Insurgent forces with ready supplies of AT mines or artillery shells could simply scale up the size of the device to maximize the blast force and fragmentation radius. The danger to the vehicle crew was often not actual penetration of the armor, but rather injuries from being thrown around the interior of a lifting or overturning vehicle. The emergency of EFPs from 2004 raised the nature of the IED threat to all Coalition vehicles. A typical example of the first crude homemade varieties consisted of a 4in-diameter copper cone powered by Composition C-4 explosive, giving an armor penetration of about 38mm at 50m, not enough to penetrate a Warrior but certainly a problem for thin-skinned vehicles. EFPs became successively more powerful and penetrative, however, particularly once the insurgents began to import professionally made examples from Iran.

As with all armored engagements throughout history, the advantages of one type of vehicle against another cannot be boiled down simply to on-paper performance comparisons. As we shall now see, the human beings manning these systems were, in many ways, the critical factor deciding who would survive a head-on encounter.

The US and the UK were not the only Coalition members to deploy armor during Operation *Iraqi Freedom*. Here we see a Ukrainian BTR-80A APC. The turret of the vehicle mounts a 14.5 × 114mm KPVT machine gun alongside a coaxial 7.62 × 54R PKT machine gun. Maximum on-road speed was up to 90km/h. (USMC)

THE COMBATANTS

IRAQ

At the time OIF was launched in 2003, about one third of Iraqi troops were regular professional soldiers or long-term reservists. The rest of the 400,000-strong army were conscripts, citizens dragged into uniform to serve in a comparatively poorly equipped and often badly led military. Iraq was still, however, a heavily militarized nation. By the late 1990s, all Iraqi citizens over the age of 18 had to undertake three years of military service, albeit with various exemptions and reductions for students and other preferential groups. It was possible to avoid conscription by paying a fee to the government, which gave the upper classes an escape route.

General conditions in the Iraqi armed forces were austere, but in some ways could be preferred to civilian life. Saddam raised military wages for many officers and men during the 1990s, effectively to buy loyalty, and at least military service kept the men from low-income labor or unemployment. But military life did bring its own set of frustrations, not least for Iraqi armor crews. Western-imposed economic sanctions bit tangibly into armored capabilities. Training times were abbreviated, especially for important matters such as live-fire trials or, crucially, combined-arms exercises. The need to preserve vehicles and conserve spares, or the simple lack of available vehicles, meant that crews had much downtime, and military reporting often simply papered over the cracks to give the appearance of effectiveness.

A fascinating insight into the endemic corruption within Iraq's armored force came to light in a post-OIF interview with a high-ranking official, transcribed in a US Classified Intelligence Report dated March 2004:

At the end of 2000, it came to Saddam's attention that approximately seventy military vehicles were immobile. Saddam told Qusay [Saddam's youngest son, who had considerable military authority] to resolve the problem. Republican Guard mechanics claimed they could repair the vehicles if the funds were made available. Qusay agreed to the work and funds were provided for the task. Once the work was completed, Qusay sent a representative to inspect the vehicles and he found them lined upon a vehicle park thirty five vehicles on each side. The vehicles looked like new, having been freshly painted and cleaned. After Qusay's representative inspected them, a second inspection was conducted to verify that they were now operational. The staff was told to supply drivers to move all vehicles to the opposite side of the vehicle park to ensure they were in working order. None of the seventy vehicles would start. When this was reported to Qusay, he instructed that Saddam not be informed, as Qusay had already told Saddam that the vehicles were operational. (Quoted in Woods 2006, p. 43–44)

A view back on the past—Iraqi armor crew and infantry mix together atop a BMP-1 during the Iran–Iraq War. Note how the vehicle has a 9M14M *Malyutka* (NATO: Sagger) ATGM mounted atop its main gun. The hull-down, dug-in position of this vehicle reflected a defensive mindset the Iraqi armored force struggled to shake over subsequent history. (Francoise De Mulder/Roger Viollet via Getty Images)

Compounding serviceability challenges for the armored crews was a general lack of coherent doctrine. Training and tactics were overwhelmingly defensive in mindset. Offensive maneuver warfare was problematic for Iraq's armed forces, culturally and practically. It required training the services could not deliver and command-and-control systems they did not possess. More important, however, was that despite efforts to develop more meritocratic and dynamic military leadership during the Iran–Iraq War, Iraq had not convincingly adopted the decentralized mission-oriented outlook of professional Western armies. The officer class still relied heavily on prescriptive and exhaustive tactical scripts, and deviation from these posed genuine risks to career and even survival—Saddam liberally ordered executions of military officers for a wildly vague spectrum of infractions. Military units also worked under

GENERAL RA'AD MAJID RASHID AL-HAMDANI

Ra'ad Majid Rashid al-Hamdani went on to have an exceptional military career within the Iraqi Republican Guard, demonstrating an equally exceptional ability to survive the political predations of Saddam Hussein's regime. He graduated from the Iraqi Military College in Baghdad in 1970 with a BA in military science. His initial military posting was as a first lieutenant in the Iraqi Army's 71st Brigade, 3d Armored Division. In this role he gained combat experience, fighting on the Golan Heights against the Israeli Defense Forces (IDF) during the 1973 Yom Kippur War. From 1977 to 1980, Hamdani became an instructor at the Iraqi Armor School and at the Iraqi Tactical School, and also studied for an MA in military science.

The outbreak of the Iran–Iraq War in 1980 saw him return to active combat service in various armored and reconnaissance forces, before moving over to the Republican Guard in 1982. During the war, he made important political connections by having Saddam's sons, Uday and Qusay, serve in his units. Hamdani became the RG's senior training officer between 1987 and 1989, after which he commanded the 17th Republican Guard Armored Brigade, and 6th Armored Division (Regular Army). He was, however, wounded in February 1991 during a Coalition air raid and spent two months in hospital. During the 1990s, Hamdani was commander of the *Al-Medina* Division (Republican Guard). He offered bold insights into the deficiencies of Iraqi military operations, but managed to survive Saddam's punishment. By the time of the OIF invasion in 2003, he was commander of II Republican Guard Corps, defending the Karbala region in central Iraq, a position that ultimately resulted in the destruction of *Al-Medina* Division. After the war, Hamdani fled the country and moved to Amman, where he has become a military academic.

General Ra'ad Majid Rashid al-Hamdani. (Public Domain)

high levels of state security surveillance, thus it was judicious for soldiers to stick to unquestioning obedience rather than independent thinking.

The top-down authority of Saddam and his odious sons sank deep through the ranks, not least in the dictator's fondness for issuing questionable doctrine. A 2002 document entitled "Training Guidance to the Republican Guard" contained the following gems from Saddam:

- train in a way that allows you to defeat your enemy;
- train all units' members in swimming;
- train your soldiers to climb palm trees so that they may use these places for navigation and sniper shooting; and
- train on smart weapons. (Woods 2006, p. 46)

Given the paucity of good tactical advice, and the constraints of leadership under Saddam's gaze, it is of little surprise that Iraqi forces were tethered to doctrines of jihadism and sacrifice, rather than intelligent innovation. This explains to a large extent why Iraqi armor crews often went static, simply digging their tanks and IFVs into large holes to act as steel pillboxes.

There were some differences, however, between the various constituents of Iraq's land forces—the regular Iraqi Army, the Republican Guard, and the Special Republican Guard (SRG). The Iraqi Army received the least investment and, apart from a few select divisions, had a patchy combat history. The RG, by contrast, was regarded as an elite (at least prior to the 1991 Gulf War), and received better wages, equipment, and status. Yet in the 1990s, the SRG effectively took over from the RG as Saddam's personal bodyguard force, as even the loyalty of the RG became doubted. The SRG was siloed from the rest of the armed forces, and unhelpfully forbidden from training and liaising with other forces, further fragmenting the possibility of coherent military operations.

The effectiveness of Iraq's armed forces was also compromised by the diversion of money and resources into Saddam's thriving private armies, which the dictator kept as an ideologically reliable insurance. The three main forces were the *Fedayeen Saddam,* the Al-Quds Army, and the Ba'ath militia. The Ba'ath militia was a ragtag collection of Saddam loyalists, typically deployed within towns and cities. "Loyalists" is a nominal label, as they were mostly absent from coherent resistance once the Coalition forces arrived. Al-Quds, by contrast, had been created in the 1990s to provide regional internal security but subsequently grew to a manpower as high as 500,000. According to post-OIF interviews, Al-Quds had scarcely any convincing capability as a military force. Its volunteer ranks received haphazard training, poor or few weapons (and often little idea of how to use them properly), few instructions about what they were meant to be doing, and they were often commanded by men with no military experience themselves. Small wonder that this force largely melted away in post-invasion Iraq.

The RPG-7 was the ubiquitous terror of Coalition armor crews during the war in Iraq. Here an Iraqi Shiite militiaman prepares his RPG-7 (which is armed with a single-stage HEAT warhead) during clashes with US Marines on August 7, 2004 in Najaf, while the insurgent beside him is readying a basic hand mortar. (Ghaith Abdul-Ahad/Getty Images)

The *Fedayeen Saddam* were a tougher proposition. Again, it was a volunteer security force, but committed to protecting against external threats as well as internal ones. Its members were ideologically fervent volunteers, who progressively built up moderate combat experience in suppression operations against Iraqi "criminals" and "saboteurs." Training was taken semi-seriously—paramilitary training camps were opened from 1994, teaching a syllabus of small-arms handling, infiltration, assassination, bombing, sabotage, reconnaissance, and surveillance. The *Saddam Fedayeen* also received some specialist kit and training from Iraqi intelligence and security services, including in advanced explosive detonators, reconnaissance unmanned aerial vehicles (UAVs), and even rocket-firing fishing boats. But membership of the *Saddam Fedayeen* was no self-indulgent Boy Scout pastime. The organization came to have extreme Sharia-like discipline within its ranks, its punishments for infractions including limb amputations and executions, somewhat offsetting the financial, educational, and employment perks that came with the group.

COALITION FORCES

The contrast between the Iraqi forces and their Coalition opponents could scarcely be more extreme. The Western forces that invaded Iraq in 2003 were a coalition in every sense of the word, a vast army that practiced as well as preached combined-arms operations at every level, all services working together under the umbrella of state-of-the-art surveillance and digital battlefield networking.

This photograph suggests the close cooperation between armor and infantry in Iraq. Here a British soldier of the 1st Battalion, The Irish Guards, is dismounted from and guarded by the Warrior seen just to the right, both providing security as engineers attempt to cap a burning oil well around Basra, April 2003. (Photo by WO2 Giles Penfound/MOD/OGL v1.0)

While we might fasten our attention on equipment differences, in many ways the critical contrast was the Coalition's culture of mission-oriented thinking, with battlefield decision-making cascading downwards to lower-ranking officers and NCOs, who had some latitude and the necessary skills to interpret and embellish their orders if it helped with mission success. Useful insight into this tactical framework for armored forces comes from the August 2002 field manual FM 3-21.71, *Mechanized Infantry Platoon and Squad (Bradley)*. The following passage shows how US Bradley crews were expected to integrate their actions with wider forces, while also taking personal responsibility for actions and outcomes:

1-1. CLOSE COMBAT

BFV [Bradley Fighting Vehicle]-equipped infantry rifle platoons and rifle squads normally operate as part of a larger force. They benefit from the support of armor, artillery, mortars, close air support, helicopters, air defense, and engineers. They also provide their own suppressive fires either to repel enemy assaults or to support their own maneuver.

a. During close combat, platoon leaders consider the following to determine how to employ the BFVs.

- Support the rifle squads with direct fires.
- Provide mobile protection to transport rifle squads to the critical point on the battlefield.
- Suppress or destroy enemy infantry fighting vehicles and other lightly armored vehicles.
- Destroy enemy armor with TOW fires.

b. Success in battle hinges on the actions of platoons, sections, and rifle squads in close combat. It also depends on their ability to react to contact; employ suppressive fires; maneuver to an enemy's vulnerable flank; and fight through to defeat, destroy, or capture an enemy. For success, the BFV-equipped infantry rifle platoon relies on the ability of leaders and soldiers to:

Here we see the gunner (bottom left) and commander of an M1A1 Abrams, the photograph taken while the tanks were conducting a counter-IED mission in Baghdad, Iraq, on December 22, 2007. Dropping down directly in front of the commander is the commander's weapon station sight. (US Army photo by Spc. Luke Thornberry)

A US Marine Corps gunnery sergeant of the 1st Tank Battalion inserts tank barrel plugs during a sandstorm near the Iraqi border in 2003. Environmental conditions were extremely hard on armor in Iraq, especially the grinding and clogging effects of the ultra-fine sand, which affected crews as much as vehicles. (Scott Nelson/Getty Images)

Just prior to the launch of Operation *Iraqi Freedom*, two crew members of an M1A1 Abrams conduct maintenance on their vehicle. A Combat Identification Panel (CIP) is mounted on the rear slat armor, this being designed to create an identifiable infrared signature when seen through thermal imaging systems. (Andy Cross/The Denver Post via Getty Images)

- Use the potential of both the rifle squads and the BFV.
- Operate their weapons with accuracy and deadly effect.
- Outthink, outmaneuver, and outfight the enemy.
- Use terrain to their advantage.

(Department of the Army 2002, 1-1–1-2)

MAJOR GENERAL GRAHAM JOHN BINNS

Major General Graham John Binns, CBE, DSO, MC, was the commander of the British 7th Armoured Brigade for the opening stages of Operation *Telic 1* in 2003. He was commissioned into the British Army's General List in 1976 before transferring to The Prince of Wales's Own Regiment of Yorkshire in 1977. As a lieutenant, then captain, in the regiment he served in Germany, Norway, and the UK, before moving to the Ministry of Defence between 1986 and 1988, then attending the Canadian Forces Command & Staff College in Toronto. His next posting was as Chief of Staff of 39 Infantry Brigade in Northern Ireland. Binns returned to The Prince of Wales's Own Regiment of Yorkshire in 1992 as commander of a Warrior company, conducting tours of the former Yugoslavia. A subsequent posting to the US Infantry School at Fort Benning in 1994 gave him wider experience of US–British cooperation, and he returned to the UK as a lieutenant colonel, serving as Directing Staff at the Army Staff College, Camberley.

The late 1990s saw Binns leading a Prince of Wales battalion on exercise in Kenya, Belize, and Canada, and on operations in Northern Ireland, before 1999, when he became Chief of Crisis Plans Branch at Headquarters Allied Forces Southern Europe and led the team responsible for NATO operational planning in the Balkans and was Chief of Staff at HQ Kosovo Force (KFOR). He assumed command of 7 Armoured Brigade in January 2001, and his leadership during *Telic* brought him the Distinguished Service Order (DSO). Subsequent roles included the Assistant Chief of Staff Commitments at Land Command and honorary Deputy Colonel of the Regiment of The Yorkshire Regiment, but in October 2006 he was appointed General Officer

Commanding 1st (UK) Armoured Division, being promoted to major general on the same day, serving in Iraq until 2008. In 2009 he took over command of the Joint Services Command and Staff College. Following retirement from the Army in 2010, he became chief executive of Aegis Defence Services, a private military and security company.

Major General Graham John Binns. (Richard Harvey, CC BY 3.0)

US and British armor crews were (and remain) the most highly trained mounted combatants in the world when it comes to the instillation of the spirit of coordinated but adaptive intelligence. In the US Army, the Military Occupational Specialty (MOS) 19K was introduced during the 1980s to designate soldiers trained to operate and maintain armored vehicles. It required intelligence, with an Armed Services Vocational Aptitude Battery (ASVAB) score of 87 in Area CO (Combat Operations), which tested linguistic skills, the ability to absorb vehicle-related information, and mechanical comprehension. The successful applicants would then go through a 15-week OSUT (One Station Unit Training) program at Fort Benning, Georgia, working through basic infantry training before Weeks 9–15 taught them proficiency as a loader, driver, and gunner on an Abrams tank. The 19D MOS training program similarly made recruits into cavalry scouts, who could then graduate to operate Bradleys and Strykers.

Gaining an armor MOS in the US Army in the early 2000s was a test of intelligence, clear thinking, and teamwork. Similar approaches to excellence were also prevalent in British armored forces. To become a Challenge 2 crew member, for example, the recruit first joined the Army as a Regular Soldier (if they were over 17 years and 1 month in age) and had to complete a 14-week basic training program. If they passed that successfully, they progressed to the Armour Centre in Bovington, Dorset, where they received 20 weeks of specialist training, working through essential driving skills before attaining a tracked vehicle license (an H license), which permitted them to go on to work inside a Challenger 2 or another armored vehicle.

Both US and British training had some important common ingredients. Unlike the Iraqi crews, Coalition armor crews had generally cross-trained through roles, meaning, for example, that a driver could step in as a loader or a gunner as a driver. This approach was not only of practical value should a crew member be injured, but it also bred faster, more intuitive crew responses in combat. The proper funding of training allowed for regular live-fire training and the use of expensive simulators and training aids, such as (in the United States) the Multiple Integrated Laser Engagement System (MILES), with unit training punctuated by major combined-arms exercises that honed skills in coordinated maneuver and adaptation to changing circumstances.

Further insight into Coalition readiness for OIF comes from the book *Heavy Metal* by Captain Jason Conroy, an account of his time as an M1A1 commander of Charlie Company, Task Force 1-64, 2d BCT, 3d ID. As a company commander, Conroy spent much of his pre-invasion deployment to Kuwait building effective teamwork through extensive live-fire exercises plus individual tank-on-tank "cage matches" using the MILES system (Conroy 2005, p. 38). Conroy notes that such single combat was not usually practiced in the tanker world, but he was inspired to do so after reading an article on the subject in *Armor* magazine. Furthermore, discussion amongst the armor community raised the possibility that the tanks might have to fight at close quarters in the cities, something that US doctrine and training had largely omitted. In response, Conroy and others scraped together useful doctrine and ideas and began running classes about how to fight in urban terrain, including factors such as obstacles, limitations to turret traverse, threat identifications, infantry cooperation, and changes to ammunition loads. His crews also invested heavily in maintenance to make sure their tanks were good to go when they had to cross the border.

What we see here is not free-wheeling independence, but rather a culture locked onto making the crews/unit as skilled and tactically aware as possible, and therefore more capable of staying on mission regardless of shifts in circumstances. As we shall see, it was what happened after the fall of Baghdad that tested their capabilities to breaking point.

A US Marine moves an APFSDS shell between M1A1 Abrams tanks in readiness for the launch of Operation *Iraqi Freedom*. The black plastic part at the top of his grip is the sabot (excluding the cap protecting the pointed shell tip), which fell away from the depleted uranium penetrator once the shell had left the muzzle. (Robert Nickelsberg/Getty Images)

COMBAT

Operation *Iraqi Freedom*, at least in terms of the initial one-month invasion, was one of the most dynamic operations in modern military history. The ground war began on March 20, 2003, and by April 14 Baghdad and most major objectives had been taken, the southern thrust of the Coalition cutting through 400km of enemy-held territory.

The armored battle was one of contrasts. Coalition MBTs and IFVs were at the spear tip of every advance, operating in a cavalry role emphasizing mobility and dynamic maneuver. Iraqi armored forces, by contrast, by and large hunkered down into their traditional defensive posture, massing heavily in places but largely opting for static firing positions. As we will here include analysis of the post-invasion insurgency, space does not allow us to expand upon every armored confrontation during OIF or the British Operation *Telic 1*. (The original British invasion was simply known as Operation *Telic*, but with subsequent deployments to Iraq the *Telic* operations were given sequential numbers.) To give clarity on the armored battle between tactics and technology, therefore, we will focus on a select number of events, setting these in an overview of the broader campaign.

INTO IRAQ

On March 20, 2003, the I MEF, UK 7th Armoured Division, and 3d ID crossed the border from Kuwait into Iraq, initially facing only light resistance. As the British troops and US Marines swung to the east to secure the Al-Faw Peninsula, the 3d ID pushed its forces through the northwest.

US Marines from Task Force *Tarawa* search an AAV for body parts and other personnel items on March 29, 2003 in the southern Iraqi city of Nasiriyah. The AAV was destroyed by RPG attacks, and many other AAVs were lost in the battle for the city. (Joe Raedle/Getty Images)

Although the Coalition quickly made brisk progress, flashpoints and centers of resistance began to emerge, in some cases producing armor vs armor and armor vs infantry engagements. It took US Marine and US Army forces from March 23 to April 2 to secure the southern city of Nasiriyah, for example, as they battled against the Iraqi Army 11th Division, which included elements of the 21st Tank Regiment and militia forces. The Iraqis, for once, used their armor to good effect. An ambush on an 18-vehicle US convoy from the 507th Maintenance Company as it drove, in error, into the city, resulted in 15 of the vehicles destroyed, including some by tank fire. (In one incident, a US Army truck was destroyed when it smashed into the traversing barrel of a Type 69-QM tank.) It was in this action that 11 US troops were killed and six captured, three male and three female soldiers, the latter famously including Private Jessica Lynch. On the same day, 18 men of Charlie Company, 1st Battalion, 2d Marines, were killed and eight Amphibious Assault Vehicles (AAVs) were destroyed as they attempted a canal bridge crossing around the city. The firepower directed upon the convoy included that from four Iraqi tanks, but the casualty list was heightened when the convoy was strafed by a US A-10 aircraft in a blue-on-blue incident. The battle for the city saw very intense street fighting, with Marine LAV cannon working hard in suppressive fire roles. An M1A1 tank was also lost in the battle, not from fire but rather after falling into the Euphrates River; all four crew drowned inside the tank.

THE ROYAL SCOTTISH DRAGOON GUARDS—OPERATION *PANZER*

Even as the US Marines and US Army were slogging it out in An Nasiriyah, the British armored forces were undergoing their own baptism of fire in the southeast of the country. The 7 Armoured Brigade had been divided into four main battlegroups, each headed by a powerful armored component:

- Royal Scots Dragoon Guards (RSDG)—30 Challenger 2s
- 2nd Royal Tank Regiment (2 RTR)—30 Challenger 2s
- The Black Watch (Royal Highland Regiment)—28 Challenger 2s
- 1st Battalion Royal Regiment of Fusiliers—28 Challenger 2s

Our focus here will primarily be on the RSDG and its key role in the struggle to secure Basra, not least in the Operation *Panzer* rescue mission fought on March 26–27 in the southern suburbs of the city.

For *Telic 1*, A Sqn, RSDG, had been assigned to the Black Watch battlegroup, B and C Sqns formed the heart of the RSDG battlegroup, while the regiment's D Sqn was divided up amongst the other squadrons. Early into the launch of *Telic 1*, A Sqn found itself heavily committed to supporting Black Watch infantry clearing the town of Az Zubayr southwest of Basra. Here Iraqi Army regulars, *Fedayeen*, and militia forces put up a vigorous close-quarters resistance using small arms, explosives, and RPGs, thus the British relied heavily upon coaxial MG fire and Warrior RARDEN fire to suppress and destroy, the tanks occasionally using high-explosive squash head (HESH) rounds to wipe out building positions or "Fin" rounds (the British shorthand for APFSDS) to punch through barriers and obstacles. During the battle, the British observed that the Iraqi defenders were learning lessons, however, realizing that the closer they moved to the British armor, the safer they were. Although the engagement was intense, the British armor emerged from it with minor casualties.

The city of Basra itself posed a more formidable objective. The principal conventional force defending the city was the 51st Mechanized Division, which included significant numbers of tanks (mainly T-55s), IFVs, and APCs. It was bolstered by *Saddam Fedayeen* and Ba'ath militia teams. Together, the Iraqis had attempted to transform Basra into something approaching a fortress city. Tanks had been dug in along expected routes of enemy approach; street obstacles were erected to channel Coalition armor and infantry into kill zones; mortars were ranged onto key target areas; vast supplies of small arms and RPGs were readied; buildings were fortified; rooftop positions established for top-down attacks on armor. The defense

An Iraqi Type 69-QM burns north of the An Numaniyah bridge on Highway 27, having been destroyed by Coalition forces in early April 2003. Many Iraqi armored vehicles were wiped out by Coalition air power, which had absolute air superiority and near-perfect situational awareness, plus plenty of precision-guided munitions. (Sgt. Paul L. Anstine II/ USMC)

was sewn together through mobile phone communications. Although the British Challenger 2s had little to fear from the individual enemy threats, collectively they posed a significant danger, especially if a tank could be disabled in narrow streets.

B Sqn, RSDG, would be used in support of the Irish Guards clearing southwest Basra, where British troops again experienced heavy street fighting. Although no tanks were lost to enemy action, on March 25 a Challenger 2 from the Queen's Royal Lancers was destroyed by a HESH round from another Challenger in a tragic act of "blue-on-blue" or "friendly fire." It was a reminder that Iraqi forces were not the only threat to Coalition armor in highly confused and dynamic battlefields.

The appropriately titled Operation *Panzer* was a C Sqn action. On March 26, the C Sqn commander, Major Johnny Biggart, was informed that 40 Commando, Royal Marines (plus elements of the Queen's Dragoon Guards), dug into defensive positions in the southern suburbs of Basra around the Shatt al-Arab waterway, were being threatened by an imminent Iraqi armored thrust, including possibly a full regiment of T-55 tanks. C Sqn's role was to make its way to the commandos across more than 30km of enemy-held territory, all while negotiating the treacherous marshlands and wide waterways, then engage and neutralize the threat in a two-pronged attack, each arm of the assault composed of two troops of tanks. There would be no infantry support for the operation. As time was of the essence, the squadron set off the same day they received their briefing.

The journey to the combat Line of Departure (LD) was as perilous as the combat itself. The Al-Faw peninsula was an armor-unfriendly zone of sucking marshland, salt flats, high banks and berms, and rusting military detritus. At one point, the 14 tanks had to cross the Shatt al-Arab waters—more than 200m wide and fast flowing—on floating and powered M3 aluminum platforms provided by the Royal Engineers, a system for which the crews had not trained, nor which had been tested in combat. Despite the complexity of the operation, all the tanks crossed successfully and by the morning of March 27 the tanks had made contact with the Royal Marines and were ready for combat on their LD.

The Iraqis, meanwhile, had been informed of the British armored threat and had turned to face A Sqn's line of approach. British reconnaissance of the terrain revealed multiple T-55s in dug-in hull-down positions, emplacing themselves along a line of raised ground to give themselves a further fire advantage. MTLB APCs, meanwhile, had brought up large numbers of Iraqi army personnel, who took up defensive positions in bunkers and trenches around the armor (Edworthy 2010, p. 141). The Iraqis had also strung numerous AT mines along the intended British lines of approach, laying them openly on the roads and tracks.

The attack went in just after dawn on March 27, the tanks following close behind a heavy preparatory artillery barrage from six self-propelled AS-90 guns of the 3rd Regiment Royal Horse Artillery. The 2nd and 3rd troops advanced together towards two road junction objectives, codenamed "Taku" and

An M1A1 Abrams tank crewman feeds a shell into the breech of the tank's 120mm gun during live-fire training. An Abrams loader would be expected to load a round in five seconds, four if he was fast. A knee-paddle switch opens the door to the ammunition store behind him. (US Army)

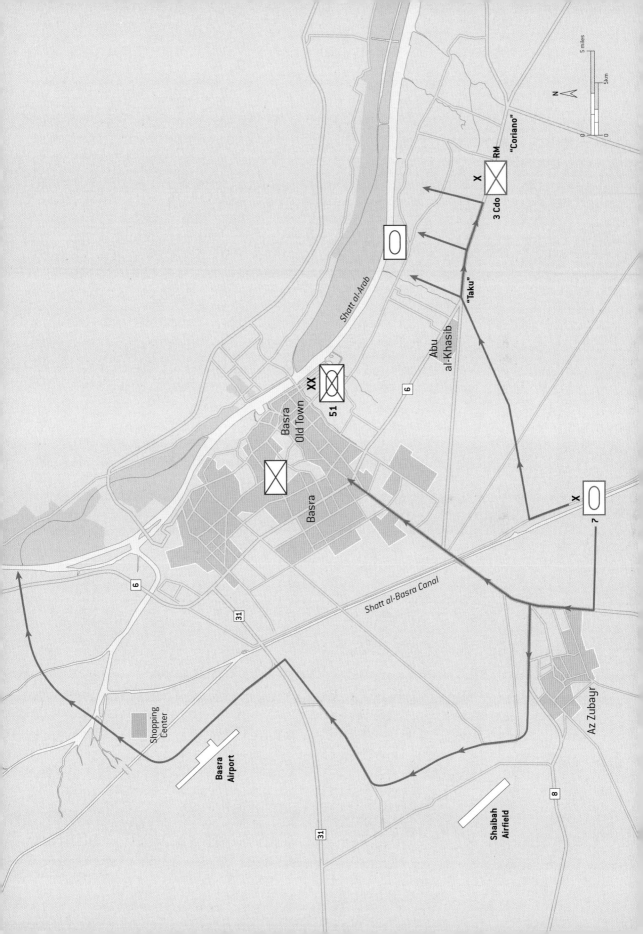

5 miles

5km

N

"Coriano"

RM

X

3 Cdo

Shatt al-Arab

Abu
al-Khasib

"Taku"

6

XX

51

Basra
Old Town

Basra

X

7

Shatt al-Basra Canal

6

31

Shopping
Center

Basra
Airport

Az Zubayr

8

Shaibah
Airfield

31

"Coriano," while 1st and 4th troops took a cross-country parallel route roughly 3km to the south, to prevent enemy movements to the east. The 3rd Troop was the first to make contact, when Captain Fraser McLeman spotted a T-55, his thermal-imaging system telling him the tank was running. Before the T-55 could send out fire, it had been destroyed by a Fin round, the ammunition brewing up and eventually blowing the tank's turret off. The tank crews then faced the tiptoe challenge of the AT mines in front of them; to handle these, they sprayed them with coaxial MG fire, which either detonated them in situ or knocked them out of the way.

Soon all the Challengers ran up against the main Iraqi defensive lines plus Iraqi armor advancing out en masse from their positions around Basra. The Iraqis opened up with everything they had, 100mm tank shells, RPGs, mortars, and heavy cannon/MG fire splitting the night. But the Challenger 2s had clear superiority of fire in the low-light conditions. With the capability to engage and destroy three targets in under ten seconds, the Challenger crews were quickly knocking out AFVs and IFVs as fast as they could fire their guns. The biggest problem proved to be that of fire discipline—there were too many target opportunities to be sure that multiple tanks weren't engaging the same targets. A partial solution was found by ordering some tanks to load only with Fin and engage the T-55s, while the others loaded with HESH and fired on softer targets.

In a matter of minutes, the Challenger 2s had destroyed seven T-55s and six MTLBs, for no losses of their own. Such was the shock and superiority imposed upon the Iraqis that their tankers began abandoning their vehicles, fleeing into the battlespace in an effort to survive. The Challengers linked up with the Commandos and Operation *Panzer* came to a successful conclusion.

C Sqn would go on to fight alongside the Commandos in a subsequent operation codenamed Operation *James*, executed on March 29–30. The operation was a combined-arms assault into southeastern Basra, focusing on the town of Abu al-Khasib. The Challengers became engaged in very intense street fighting, albeit without the armor engagements of *Panzer*. One notable incident, however, occurred when 3rd Troop came across 14 Iraqi tanks, abandoned in their defensive positions. To prevent the vehicles from being put back into use in the future, the Challengers destroyed all 14 vehicles with 120mm rounds.

TASK FORCE 1-64 AND THE BATTLE OF MAHMUDIYAH

Focusing again on the US effort, the struggle in Nasiriyah was soon joined by other city battles, especially at Karbala and An Najaf. One of the key formations engaged at this time was TF 1-64, 2d BCT, 3d ID, which had been driving hard through the southwestern Iraqi desert since the launch of OIF. It was divided into two main elements: "Heavy Metal," which contained all the brigade's heavy armor (70 M1A1s and 60 Bradleys), and "Rock 'n Roll," all the BCT's wheeled vehicles. It was heading towards Baghdad directly into the face of the RG *Al-Medina* Division, which was

estimated to have 211 tanks, 293 APCs, and 69 towed artillery pieces (Conroy 2005, p. 68–69), a worryingly unequal order of battle for the US armor crews.

Resistance to TF 1-64's advance through Iraq soon stiffened. Attacks were delivered with a variety of tactical approaches—small-arms ambushes, mortar barrages, RPG sniping or mass volleys, light vehicle attacks, but relatively little in the way of enemy armor. In fact, the heavy Iraqi armor was concentrated in the hands of the *Al-Medina* and *Nebuchadnezzar* divisions, which were emplaced farther north around the approaches to Baghdad, particularly around the "Karbala Gap" about 40km to the southwest of Baghdad.

But there were still many threats for 1-64. During a push to secure bridges in An Najaf on March 26, multiple Abrams, Bradleys, and other vehicles were hit by blistering RPG and small-arms fire, although in return the US armor helped destroy 30 Iraqi vehicles of every description, including BMPs. On the approach to Karbala, 1-64 ran into more Iraqi armor, in the process claiming seven more BMPs and eight armed trucks. It was becoming clear that it was almost suicidal for Iraqi tanks and IFVs to try to take on the US armor. Bradleys were also beginning to make tank kills, as the 25mm AP ammunition was capable of punching through BMPs and the lighter Iraqi MBTs.

One of the most famous 1-64 armor engagements, however, occurred on April 3, when the 2d BCT attacked into Mahmudiyah, a suburb about 25km south of Baghdad where armor had been reported. In fact, the *Al-Medina* Division had deployed T-72s into the streets, the best of Iraqi armor serving as an ambush force in the close confines of the streets. The primary US units sent into the town were Charlie Company, TF 1-64, a "heavy" company (known by the codename "Cobra") of 14 M1A1s and a Bradley for fire support, and Charlie Company, TF 3-15 ("Charlie Rock"), a mechanized infantry company bolstered with a platoon of Abrams tanks.

The approach and initial penetration into Mahmudiyah in the late afternoon hours brought increasing resistance from small arms and RPG attacks, especially from

This M1A1 Abrams of Bravo Company, 2d Tank Battalion, USMC, was destroyed by cumulative insurgent fire near Sayyid Abd, Iraq, in April 2003. Although the survivability of the Abrams was generally good, there were some identified vulnerabilities to side and rear armor, eventually addressed in the TUSK upgrade. (MSGT Howard J. Farrell/USMC)

PREVIOUS PAGES: T-72s vs
M1A1s, Mahmudiyah, Iraq, April
3, 2003.
On the afternoon of April
3, 2003, the M1A1s of Charlie
Company, TF 1-64, advanced into
Mahmudiyah, there being reports
of Iraqi armor in the city. The lead
tank in the company,
commanded by SSgt Randy
Pinkston, suddenly found itself
facing two T-72s parked in a
narrow street, one with its gun
pointing away, the other towards
the US tank. The tanks were first
spotted by the tank's gunner, Sgt
Scott Stewart, who reported the
vehicles to his commander.
Pinkston immediately responded
by initiating an engagement
sequence, requesting that the
loader, Pfc Artemio Lopez, load a
sabot round. However, a HEAT
round was in the breech and was
fired at the tank on the right,
slicing through its thinner rear
armor and utterly destroying it,
the explosion blowing off its
turret. The T-72 on the left
responded, firing a 125mm shell
at the US tank, but it flew high
and hit a building behind. The US
tank engaged this vehicle, but
again a HEAT was loaded and
fired, striking the T-72's thicker
turret armor with little visible
effect. The M1A1 directly behind
Pinkston's tank had by this time
moved up in support, and fired a
sabot round that punched
through the Iraqi vehicle's armor
and blew the T-72 apart.

A Challenger 2 tank rolls through
Az Zubayr in early April 2003, the
loader manning the pintle-
mounted 7.62 × 51mm L7A2
machine gun. Either side of the
main gun are clusters of
multibarrel grenade smoke
grenade dischargers, loaded with
L8 smoke grenades for putting
down heavy obscuration in an
instant. (Angus Beaton/MOD/
Getty Images)

elevated building positions (Mahmudiyah had many three- or four-story houses), so
the armor crews had to remain under closed hatches, engaging targets with coaxial
MG fire. Then the lead tank in Cobra found itself facing two T-72s parked next to
one another in a narrow street—both tanks were destroyed in quick succession (see
artwork commentary).

At this moment, however, the driver of another M1A1 spotted a T-72 parked in an
alley to his right, about 25ft away. The M1A1 turret was frantically traversed, and a
sabot round fired, even though the Iraqi tank was so close the gunner could not get
visual target acquisition. The shell destroyed the T-72, again blowing its turret off. As
the unit moved on, another Abrams crew identified a T-72 close by in a side street,
performing another ultra-fast firing cycle that again resulted in a turretless T-72.

Over the following minutes, three more T-72s were added to the list of close-
range kills, totaling seven T-72s for no losses. Charlie Company also destroyed two
BMPs that attempted to get into the fight. As this tank-on-tank action was taking
place, the Bradleys of Charlie Rock were playing their part, hacking at buildings
with 25mm fire to destroy enemy insurgents. One interesting point to emerge from
the OIF street battles, however, was that the Bradleys often could not elevate their
guns sufficiently to engage targets in very high positions (the elevation of an M2A2
ODS was 57°), whereas infantry traveling in M113 APCs could engage these targets.
The Mahmudiyah tank engagement, however, reported in full in Jason Conroy's
book *Heavy Metal*, perfectly illustrates the superiority of US armor and crews over
Iraq armor in OIF.

On the same day that 1-64 was battling through Mahmudiyah, the Iraqi 10th
Armored Brigade from the *Al-Medina* Division and the 22nd Armored Brigade from
the *Nebuchadnezzar* Division made a major counterattack against the American
bridgehead at Musayib, during what is known as the Battle of the Karbala Gap. The
night attack on April 2–3 was roundly savaged by US airpower and tank gunnery. A
Troop, 3d Sqn, 7th Cav Reg alone destroyed 12 tanks, three ZSU self-propelled antiaircraft guns, and one towed howitzer. Bradleys blasted apart dozens of trucks, jeeps,
and civilian vehicles bringing Iraqi troops and militia into the fight. By the end of the

battle, the *Al-Medina* Division had effectively ceased to exist. As with earlier engagements, in many cases the US gunners found the Iraqi tanks static in dug-in positions; once identified, they were destroyed at will.

THE INSURGENCY

By April 9, 2003, the Coalition forces had penetrated to the center of Baghdad and the regime had fallen. Consolidation and security operations continued throughout the capital and the country for several more days, but it appeared that to a large extent "Major combat operations in Iraq have ended," as President George W. Bush famously declared on the deck of the aircraft carrier USS *Abraham Lincoln* on May 1, 2003. As history now knows, it was not to be. The vacuum left by the collapse of Saddam Hussein's regime, the lack of effective governmental replacement, and the disbandment of the Iraqi armed forces created an incubator for extremism and insurgency, unleashing horrific violence against the Coalition presence, escalating at times to outright urban warfare.

For Coalition armor crews, the insurgency changed everything. The Iraqi insurgents could now orientate RPG and IED attacks against vehicles with greater planning, preparation, and ingenuity, and at times and locations of their choosing. With IEDs, furthermore, the insurgents didn't even need to be present to destroy armored opponents.

During the invasion phase of OIF, Coalition armor casualties had been very light indeed. But during the insurgency, they began to mount rapidly, with damage or kills becoming an almost daily occurrence. A random selection of fatal incidents from one month, September 2005, proves the point:

- **September 2**—A Bradley M3A2 of 3 Sqn, 7th Cav, is hit by an IED, killing a crew member.

The fighting in Sadr City in 2004 required large volumes of heavy armor on the streets to dominate the militia forces. Here we see Abrams tanks covering opposite sides of the street and a Bradley (in the background) working under the cover of an AH-64 Apache attack helicopter. (KARIM SAHIB/AFP via Getty Images)

- **September 16**—Three 4-64 Armor M1A1 crew members are killed when their tank is hit by an IED in Baghdad.
- **September 19**—A roadside bomb destroys an M2A2 BFV near Ramadi.
- **September 28**—Five soldiers are killed when their Bradley M2A2 was attacked by "indirect fire" (according to casualty reports) in Ramadi.

Selecting any other month from the casualty lists presents a similar picture. What these figures do not show, however, was that the losses amongst armored vehicle crews were far, far below those suffered by infantry and other soldiers operating within light armed vehicles, especially Humvees. The September 2005 data show at least 23 US soldiers killed by IEDs when traveling in Humvees, trucks, or light armored vehicles, such as M113s. Thus, while heavier armor was taking casualties, it was still a safer prospect than light vehicles.

FORCE MULTIPLIER

The insurgency in Iraq prompted a live rewriting of Western armored warfare doctrine. The incessant RPG and IED attacks proved that even the heaviest AFVs were vulnerable; there is video footage of M1A1s being lifted many meters into the air by under-belly IED detonations. But Coalition MBTs and IFVs also continued to provide the protected firepower and troop movement that became essential in large-scale anti-insurgent operations.

On November 7, 2004, for example, the Coalition forces (which now included some units of the reborn Iraqi Army) began a ferocious six-week battle to break the

A USMC Amphibious Assault Vehicle (AAV) conducts a breaching operation for Marines assigned to 2d Platoon, India Company, 3d Battalion, 1st Marines, 1st Marine Division, during actions in Fallujah in November 2004. The AAV attracted some controversy in Iraq, with relatively high losses leading to some labelling it as one of the vulnerable pieces of armor in the US inventory. (US Marines photo by Lance Cpl. Ryan L. Jones)

insurgent grip over the city of Fallujah, 110km to the west of Baghdad. It became the largest, and costliest, city battle in the post-invasion phase of OIF. Although it was in essence a counterinsurgency operation, heavy armor was deployed by both the Marine Corps and the Army—M1A1s, M1A2s, Bradleys, LAV-25s, and Strykers would be used en masse. Against them was a force of between 1,000 and 3,000 insurgents of various affiliations. They had extensively prepared the city for defense, including lacing the streets with ready-emplaced IEDs for the expected armored assault.

The subsequent battle proved yet again that armor had a vital role in urban combat. The insurgents' prepared defenses and knowledge of the streets often put the Marines and Army infantry at a disadvantage in the street fighting, but they took a true combined-arms approach, maneuvering with the support of heavy tank and cannon fire. Plough fittings on Abrams tanks delivered swift obstacle clearance. The insurgents were learning, however. As the battle went on, US forces increasingly observed that the insurgents would refrain from engaging US armor until it had passed by, before unleashing their fire on the infantry following the vehicles for cover. It was also noted that when the insurgents did attack AFVs, they adjusted their targeting, aiming for tracks, bore evacuator, and optics—destroying or mangling these more easily damageable components could effectively result in a disability kill. An official US Marine history of the battle also observed tactical differences between Marine and Army use of MBTs:

An LAV-25 patrols the city of Fallujah in November 2004. Fallujah was the scene of some of the US military's most intense urban combat since the battle of Hue, Vietnam, in 1968. The LAV proved itself as a versatile force multiplier, but it was vulnerable to RPG and IED attacks. (MEHDI FEDOUACH/AFP via Getty Images)

> As the battle unfolded, one could see the different ways Marines and soldiers utilized their M1A1 and M1A2 tanks, with the key difference being that Marine tanks continuously accompanied Marine infantrymen during deliberate clearing operations, whereas Lieutenant Colonel Rainey's tanks [belonging to the Army's TF 2-7] generally held positions along the main line of communication after their initial assault. (McWilliams 2014, p. 25)

Strykers were also proving themselves alongside the Bradleys. Their speed of movement was demonstrated to be a real asset in Fallujah and beyond, not only for the rapidity with which they could deploy to and extract from hot spots, but also because they had the capability to chase, catch, and detain enemy vehicles, something the Bradley struggled to achieve. They did, however, appear vulnerable to damage from enemy fire (see Analysis chapter).

The British also discovered the value of armor in their own insurgency efforts. The Warrior in particular became the fighting workhorse of choice, recommending itself

Conveying the devastating power of the Abrams' 120mm main gun, this photograph shows a USMC M1A1 of the 2d Tank Battalion destroying a building in Fallujah, Al-Anbar Province, in December 2004. The optimal round for urban combat was found to be the M830A1 MPAT, which could be used for both antitank and antimateriel functions, with multiple fuzing options. (Lance Cpl. James J. Vooris/USMC)

An Iraqi protester throws stones at a burning British Warrior set on fire by petrol bombs during clashes in the southern Iraqi city of Basra on September 19, 2005. The crew had to abandon the vehicle, with their clothes in flames. (ESSAM AL-SUDANI/AFP via Getty Images)

through survivability and firepower. Two of the most famous Warrior incidents were those involving Private Johnson Gideon Beharry, a Warrior driver in the 1st Battalion, Princess of Wales's Royal Regiment (PWRR). On May 1, 2004, Beharry's company was moving through the contentious city of Al-Amarah to resupply the isolated British CIMIC-House command outpost. During the movement, however, it was retasked with extracting a British foot patrol under attack. Beharry was the driver in his platoon commander's vehicle. As the vehicle came to a stop on a suspiciously quiet street, it was suddenly hit by multiple RPGs, the explosions wounding the Warrior's commander and gunner and also some of the dismounted infantry in the back. All the vehicle's radio communications went down.

Beharry decided to drive the vehicle himself out of the kill zone, but as he maneuvered the Warrior was hit several more times by RPGs, setting it on fire and filling the interior with smoke. In response, Beharry threw open his driver's hatch to gain better visibility and guided the vehicle around an enemy road barricade, thus providing directional guidance to the five other vehicles of the platoon behind him. Further RPG hits destroyed his hatch and he was struck in the helmet by a 7.62mm round. In his perilous state, with the vehicle still burning, he managed to reach CIMIC-House, where

An M1A1 tank commander from Charlie Company, 1-64, 3d ID, keeps careful watch during a patrol in a southeastern neighborhood of Baghdad on October 11, 2005. Directly in front of him is the Commander's Weapon Station Sight and his left hand is operating the Commander's Control Handle. (DAVID FURST/AFP via Getty Images)

An Abrams tank burns to destruction after being hit by an IED in eastern Baghdad on March 10, 2006. Abrams tanks suffered heavily in Iraq. US Army Major General Terry Tucker stated in February 2005 that of 1,100 Abrams tanks that had seen service in Iraq, 70 percent had received significant combat damage. (Akram Saleh/Getty Images)

he stopped outside and pulled his commander and gunner to safety, before helping the dismounted troops to cover.

The incident in May 2004 would not be the last in Beharry's eventful military career. On June 11 of the same year, Beharry's platoon was again ambushed in Al-Amarah, multiple RPGs hitting his vehicle, including one that left him with a serious head injury and wounded his commander and several other occupants. He again managed to maneuver his vehicle and the occupants to relative safety before passing out from his injuries.

Beharry was awarded the Victoria Cross (VC) for his cumulative bravery in 2004. Respectfully putting his actions aside, however, we can see how durable the Warrior was in terms of riding out RPG hits and staying functional. During the defense of CIMIC-House, which found itself under frequent attack and even siege conditions, the Warrior provided invaluable support, not just in terms of heavy firepower but also, according to one British ops officer, Steve Brooks, for "assault, casevac, comms relay, extraction, escorts, VCPs [vehicle checkpoints], intimate support—everything" (quoted in Holmes 2006, p. 270).

Brooks makes an important point that

RPG ATTACK, BASRA, 2004

Here we see an insurgent's viewpoint through the 2.8× PGO-7 optic of an RPG-7, as he targets a British Warrior FV510 IFV on the outskirts of Basra in 2004. The square grid at the top of the reticle is intended for use with HE-Frag and HEAT rounds, with the numbers 2, 3, 4, and 5 giving elevation in hundreds of meters; the two "+" symbols above the grid denote (from top to bottom) 50m and 100m range. The boxes to the left and right of the central double line are used for calculating windage. The continuation of the double line below the grid is for use with tandem-charge warheads (heavier, therefore requiring more elevation)—again, 1, 1.5, and 2 are providing ranges in hundreds of meters. The curved line right of center, marked 2–10, is a stadiametric rangefinder, based on an average armored vehicle being 2.7m tall. By placing the vehicle so that its tracks/wheels sit on the baseline and the turret just touches the curved line, the user is able to estimate the range with reasonable accuracy.

can be generalized beyond the Warrior. In an urban insurgency, Coalition forces found that armor was one of its greatest assets, despite the vulnerabilities of different vehicle types. Armor created a firepower force multiplier, while IFVs provided a protected environment for transporting small units of infantry to and from engagements. (More about the virtues, and weaknesses, of armor in Iraq will be discussed in the next section.) But at the same time, hard lessons were being learned about armor's vulnerability to RPGs and large IEDs. Therefore between 2004 and 2006 we see the increasing investment in field modifications and upgrades to armor packages, to improve survivability under the adaptive and probing attacks of the insurgent forces. These measures did not stop vehicles being lost over subsequent years, but they did improve the survivability of crews and occupants.

ANALYSIS

Looked at from any angle, there was a profound asymmetry between the combatants in Operation *Iraqi Freedom*. The Coalition represented one of the most powerful armed forces assembled since World War II, the cutting edge of training, technology, and tactics, supremely confident in its own capabilities to get the tactical job done. On the other side was Iraq, its military a depleted, politicized, and leaden organization, institutionally and psychologically damaged from years of warfare and political repression. It had, however, spawned a deep structure of paramilitary and militia forces which, despite the decidedly sketchy nature of their training and tactical capabilities, went on to cause long-term problems far greater than the challenge of overcoming Iraq's official military forces. In conventional warfare, Iraq's land forces were completely overmatched and outmaneuvered, which was witnessed tragically in the unequal battles between Coalition armored vehicles and Iraq's creaking fleet of AFVs. But in the insurgency that followed, Iraq's paramilitaries managed to find literal and metaphorical gaps in the Coalition armor. Thus, the coalition armor crews found themselves fighting in a war for which they had not prepared, taking armor into street-level battles that would change the nature of modern armored warfare doctrine.

COMBAT PERFORMANCE

Assessing the initial invasion phase (March 20–May 1, 2003), the Coalition forces came off particularly well in terms of armored vehicle losses. Within the US Army's V Corps, only 23 M1A1 Abrams and M2/M3 Bradleys were actually penetrated by enemy fire, with very few personnel losses. Most of the damage was caused by 12.7mm

US soldiers from the 1st Cavalry Division, 2d Battalion, 7th Cavalry, dismount from a Bradley M2A3 fighting vehicle and take up position during an offensive operation in Najaf on August 15, 2004. The infantry moves quickly to cover against the side of the street, while the Bradley remains in the center, ready to deliver heavy support fire. (Joe Raedle/ Getty Images)

MG fire, cannon fire from AA guns or BMP-2s, or by RPGs striking vulnerable parts of the tanks, such as external fuel containers, engine compartments, or thinner side-skirt armor. On the British side, the loss figures were even more modest. Only a single Challenger 2 had been destroyed, by friendly tank fire. Of the Coalition vehicles hit by RPGs, in the majority of cases the AFVs were not destroyed, but minor initial damage could expand to become an outright kill. During the battle for Baghdad in early April 2003, for example, just two Abrams were disabled by engine fires after being hit by multiple projectiles, the tanks being destroyed by US tanks and combat helicopters to prevent their access by the enemy. Bradley losses were also often the result of external fires spreading from bustle racks to engine compartments. Many AVFs survived with little more than scratches and indentations, however, despite being struck multiple times.

On the Iraqi side, of course, the picture was radically different. Accurate data is impossible to come by, but most estimates circle around the figure of 3,300 Iraqi AFVs destroyed in 2003 by all causes. While a large (likely a majority) percentage of these kills came from air attack, hundreds were certainly destroyed by Coalition armor. The reasons for the disproportionate figures are multiple, but include:

- More professional Coalition AFV crews, with better tactical training, faster gunnery responses, and more intelligent tactics, the latter especially in the realm of combined-arms maneuvers with infantry, artillery, and air power.
- Superior Coalition vehicle technologies, particularly with regard to fire control, night vision, communications, and situational awareness. Of the FBCB2 system, for example, Cpt Stewart James, Commander, A Company, 2d Battalion, 69th Armor, said that "You have just reduced layers of friction, and the fog of war is why units lose. This is simultaneous, real-time synchronization. It reduces the friction of war about a hundredfold" (Conatser & Grizio 2005, p. 41).
- Poor or non-existent tactical decision-making among the Iraqi armor formations, which in many cases adopted traditional defensive postures that were disastrous

against a highly professional and mobile enemy with excellent overhead surveillance.

- Poor levels of training amongst Iraqi armor crews, leading to slow response times and a lack of coordination between vehicles and other arms of service.
- A rapid Iraqi collapse of centralized command and control, leading to many armor crews simply abandoning their vehicles once it became apparent that they were leaderless and outclassed.

DOCTRINE AND DEPLOYMENT

As we saw in the Combat chapter, however, the balance of advantage shifted against the armor in many senses during the subsequent insurgency. One particularly insightful analysis of the US armor experience during OIF comes from an After Action Review written by Cpt Larry Burris of TM C/3-15 Infantry, TM 1-64, submitted on 24 April 2003. This lengthy document (links to it are provided in the Bibliography) makes circumspect observations and recommendations about the technical and tactical performance of armor in OIF. Despite being written little more than a month after the initial invasion, Burris' opening points are relevant to both the invasion and the subsequent insurgency, and are worth quoting at length:

> The current doctrinal manuals on Urban Operations do not address how best to utilize armored forces in an urban environment. The enemy faced by this unit hid his tanks and vehicles under camouflaged covers, beneath bridge overpasses, inside of buildings on narrow streets, and under low trees. These enemy systems were not seen until they were only meters away. No degree of IPB [intelligence preparation of the battlefield] could compensate, alert, or prepare any US force for the massive numbers of RPGs stored in houses, shacks, lockers, and cars.

Multiple mortar shells have here been fused together using detcord (which has been cut by ordnance disposal personnel) to create a powerful daisy-chain IED. The device was part of a haul discovered in central Baghdad, including ordnance buried in the grounds of Abbas Mosque in the Ameriya district. (Michael Macor/ The San Francisco Chronicle via Getty Images)

The only way to counter RPGs fired from covered and concealed positions was to absorb the hit, identify the source of the fire, and respond with massive overwhelming firepower.

Tanks and Bradleys repeatedly sustained hits from RPG's and ground directed anti aircraft fire that dismounted infantrymen, HMMWVs and other light skinned vehicles could not sustain. Bradleys successfully protected the infantrymen inside while at the same time delivering a massive volume of fire against dismounted enemy, trucks, tanks, and armored vehicles. The firepower and shock generated by tanks and Bradleys could never have been matched by dismounted infantry. Without the use of these systems initially, the enemy would have caused many more casualties.

(Burris 2003)

Burris' essential message is that the US Army was tactically unprepared for the deployment of armor into urban zones, but that armor nevertheless had a critical positive impact for reducing casualties and gaining fire superiority.

The value of armor meant that it was quickly in high demand, a reality explored in more detail by a 2005 article in *Joint Force Quarterly* revealingly titled "'Everybody Wanted Tanks': Heavy Forces in Operation *Iraqi Freedom*". The six key reasons given for the popularity of tanks in urban battles are:

1. Tanks were highly resistant to fire.
2. Tanks led the advance.
3. Tanks immediately took the enemy under fire.
4. Tanks were highly effective in urban operations.

Not all armor casualties were due to enemy fire. Accidents also claimed many vehicles damaged or even destroyed. This Bradley lies on its side after a mechanical problem caused it to slide off the road and tip over on its side. (KARIM SAHIB/AFP via Getty Images)

"DAISY-CHAIN" IED ATTACK

The daisy-chain method of IED attack was particularly effective at hitting Coalition vehicle convoys, as its explosive force could be directed along tens or even hundreds of meters of distance, maximizing the opportunities for vehicle kills despite the convoy practicing recommended distancing. Rather than emplacing an IED at a single location, the daisy-chain method used multiple devices placed at intervals along the route of travel, here an urban carriageway, but connected for simultaneous detonation by using detonating cord. In Iraq, the classic daisy-chain devices were 155mm artillery shells (with fuse caps removed and detcord inserted), mortar shells, or AT mines, the explosives hidden at the side of the road, or beneath its surface, and often heavily disguised with garbage, industrial materials, dead animals, etc. In some advanced attacks, the IEDs were placed inside plaster-of-paris kerbstones specifically cast around the shells. The daisy-chain IED was typically detonated when as many targets as possible were inside the kill zone, sometimes optimized by placing a supposedly broken-down vehicle across the road to slow the vehicles, bunch them up, and channel them closer to the devices. Detonation came via mechanisms such as command wires or, more commonly as the insurgency wore on, signals from an operator with a cellular phone, "calling" another phone attached to the detonator of one of the IEDs. Later in the insurgency, explosively formed projectiles (EFPs) were seen daisy-chained specifically for antiarmor effects.

Bradley M2A2 vehicles receive a much-needed clean-down in Kuwait following operations in Iraq. The Bradley came out of OIF with its reputation reinforced. Not only was it a capable infantry support platform, but it had also showed that it could fight and win in battles against Soviet-era armor. (YASSER AL-ZAYYAT/AFP via Getty Images)

5. Tanks had shock effect.
6. Fuel supply was less of a problem than originally thought.

(Gordon & Pirnie 2005, p. 85–86)

The authors went on to highlight some important distinctions between the tactical use of MBTs and IFVs in OIF. Often, the cannon firepower of IFVs like the Bradley and the Warrior was "more appropriate than the main guns of tanks" because it could switch easily between antipersonnel and antivehicle fire, plus had better elevation and depression to engage a wider vertical radius of targets. As a general rule, "The automatic cannons and grenade launchers of the infantry fighting vehicles were also excellent against lightly constructed buildings. Against better-built, larger structures, tank main guns, aircraft-delivered weapons, or artillery were more useful" (Gordon & Pirnie 2005, p. 88).

SURVIVAL

On the issue of protection, however, Burris, Gordon, and Pirnie note the vulnerabilities of armor against mass RPG and IED environments. Burris cites as an issue "The lack of adequate armor on the flanks of Bradley and Tank turrets and hulls" (Burris 2003), resulting in crews having to improvise external armor (although Burris saw ERA tiles as the optimal solution). Gordon and Pirnie argued that "While RPG-7 rounds would only rarely penetrate tanks, infantry fighting vehicles were far more vulnerable" (Gordon & Pirnie 2005, p. 87), especially to HEAT rounds (HE warheads were incapable of penetrating the armor). Such is certainly borne out in the figures, for while 23 Abrams were lost in the entire conflict, approximately 150 Bradleys were destroyed from a variety of causes.

Yet as we saw in the Design and Development chapter, the war in Iraq prompted major survivability upgrades to US armor, and these began to bear fruit. Seemingly crude additions like slat armor, designed to weaken the particle jet of shaped charges,

US Marines from Regimental Combat Team-1 (RCT-1) conduct security patrols during the national elections in January 2005. Note how the infantry and the M1A1 Abrams work very closely together. If the unit was ambushed, the tank would be used for heavy fire suppression, position destruction, and building breaching (if collateral damage considerations allowed). (Regimental Combat Team-1 Combat Camera/USMC)

dramatically increased the prospects of surviving RPG strikes, for example. In an article in 2005, Maj Nicholas Mullen, rear detachment commander of the 1st Brigade, 25th Infantry Division—a Stryker BCT—noted that while most were initially skeptical over the slat armor, combat experience quickly won them over. He remembers one slat-armor-equipped Stryker being hit by three RPGs with little damage to the core vehicle or those inside (Jean 2005).

Vehicles would continue to be lost in Iraq to RPGs and IEDs over the duration of the conflict, which effectively ended in 2011 (although violence in Iraq continues to this day). But what was certain was that armor had proven its value, despite operating in what was its most hostile environment.

A Bradley M2A2 ODS of the 1st Battalion, 22d Regiment, 4th Infantry Division, secures the perimeter of its target area during a raid in Tikrit, the hometown of Saddam Hussein, in January 2004. With the heavy presence of Coalition combat aviation above, the vehicle is fitted with Combat Identification Panels. (JEWEL SAMAD/AFP via Getty Images)

AFTERMATH

Coalition armor was deployed, in some form, until the final withdrawal of major Western forces in 2011. Until the tanks and IFVs pulled out, they continued to fight, and equally continued to be destroyed, albeit in reduced numbers.

In the spring of 2008, for example, US and British armor crews battled against the Mahdi Army militia at flashpoints across Iraq, including Sadr City, Kut, Nasiriyah, and Basra. In Sadr City, the heavier armor of the 1st Combined Arms Battalion, 68th Armored Regiment (1-68 CAB) and the 1st Squadron, 2nd Stryker Cavalry Regiment (1-2 SCR), took the brunt of much of the effort to quash the insurgents. In the build-up to the action, the focus for 1-68 CAB had been mostly on using up-armored Humvees, working in teams of four vehicles and 16–20 soldiers. But the intensity of the close-quarters fights quickly returned the battalion to M1 Abrams and M2 Bradleys as their lead elements, the patrols being reorganized based around one Bradley and two Abrams, or two Bradleys and one tank, with dismounted and Humvee-mobile infantry in support (Spencer 2019). The armor performed well, but there were also hard lessons to be learned. In this battle, for example, the Strykers seemed more vulnerable to the RPGs and new generations of EFPs being deployed against them than the Bradleys and Abrams, with 1-2 SCR losing six Strykers in as many days (Spencer 2019).

Battles such as that which occurred in Sadr City all fed into wider doctrinal debates about the future of armor, arguments that continue to this day. Roughly splicing the contentions, on one side are those who contend that heavy armor's place in modern warfare is assured, not least because its role in urban combat was proven in Iraq. Others, however, see the days of MBTs and heavy IFVs as numbered, to be consigned to history by the ever-rising capabilities of ATGMs and other tank-killing systems (such as armed drones), plus the greater importance of mobility to respond quickly to

distant threats. They point to the armor losses in Iraq and many other recent conflicts as proof of tank/IFV vulnerabilities.

The discussions (which admittedly have many more shades and hues than those presented here) are not mere abstract arguments. In 2020, for example, the USMC announced that it was getting rid of its heavy armor, sending most of its Abrams tanks over to Army stocks as it sought to transform its expeditionary capabilities. There has been much debate over upgrade or replacement programs for individual vehicles, framed by the wider doctrinal disputes. One of the most tortuous has been the UK's Warrior Capability Sustainment Programme (CSP), an international effort running since the early 2000s to upgrade Warrior's firepower to a fully stabilized 40mm cannon, with concomitant upgrades to its systems. After huge effort, testing, competition, and financial outlay, the UK's Ministry of Defence (MOD) announced in March 2021 that the program was to be canceled, the focus instead shifting to the acquisition of the wheeled Boxer IFV. In the United States, the US Army is looking towards the eventual replacement of the Bradley through the Optionally Manned Fighting Vehicle (OMFV) program. As the program name suggests, the winning vehicle will have the capability to operate with a crew or without, the latter via remote control or in autonomous mode. The OMFV is part of the wider Next Generation

With supreme irony, these M1A1M Abrams tanks are in Iraqi Army service in 2011, as part of a major transfer of armor between the United States and the new Iraqi state. The export versions of the M1A1 have the Export Armor Package (EAP), which does not feature depleted-uranium armor. (Daneille Hendrix/US Army)

Combat Vehicle (NGCV), which is also looking to replace the M1 Abrams, although the form that replacement will take has yet to settle. In 2022, however, General Dynamics introduced the AbramsX technology demonstrator, a radically re-envisaged Abrams with (as much as details allow) a smaller crew (via an autoloader), new gun, active-protection system, and other advancements. As a demonstrator, its future as a production or service vehicle has yet to be decided, but some enthusiastic pundits have said that it could see the Abrams live on through the 2050s. The British, meanwhile, are pushing ahead with a redesigned Challenger, the Challenger 3, with an improved hull and a shift to the 120mm L55A1 smoothbore gun.

While the Western Coalition nations were wrangling with their armored futures, post-OIF Iraq was taking a different route as it rebuilt its forces. On December 19, 2014, for example, the US Defense Security Cooperation Agency announced the following export sale:

> The State Department has made a determination approving a possible Foreign Military Sale to Iraq for M1A1 Abrams tanks and associated equipment, parts and logistical support for an estimated cost of $2.4 billion. The Defense Security Cooperation Agency delivered the required certification notifying Congress of this possible sale today. The Government of Iraq has requested a possible sale of 175 Full Track M1A1 Abrams Tanks with 120mm Gun modified and upgraded to the M1A1 Abrams configuration.
>
> (DSCA 2014)

Now Iraq would be operating Abrams armor, not fighting against it. The export Abrams would also see heavy fighting against insurgent groups, including the formidable Islamic State in the Levant (ISIL). The experience was mixed. While the tanks undoubtedly added combat power, the vehicles—which were not equipped with the DU armor of the US tanks—proved vulnerable to ATGMs (new generations were being exported to the insurgents from Iran and Syria), RPGs, EFPs, and IEDs, with 28 tanks being significantly damaged in 2014. Interestingly, the United States was later compelled to place restrictions upon Iraqi use of the Abrams after some of the tanks fell into the hands of Iranian-backed militias, but in response, in 2018 an Iraqi brigade (the 38th Armored) responded by taking delivery of 39 Russian T-90S tanks.

The Iraq War had a shaping influence on the future of armored warfare. If anything, it proved that armor's value (or otherwise) is an inextricable fusion of technology, training, and tactics. The most advanced vehicle on the market will become battlefield debris if not used intelligently by highly trained users. Regarding the evolution of armor, it is as much as matter of people and training as it is about the vehicles themselves.

BIBLIOGRAPHY

Bashista, Ronald J. (1991). "War Revives Armor Badge Issue." *Armor*, July–August 1991.

Below the Turret Ring (June 13, 2015). "The armor protection of the T-72 tank": https://below-the-turret-ring.blogspot.com/2015/06/the-armor-protection-of-t-72-tank.html

Burris, Capt Larry Q. (April 24, 2003). "Operation *Iraqi Freedom* After Action Review Comments." Department of the Army, Team C, 3d Battalion, 15th Infantry Regiment: https://www.blackfive.net/main/2003/09/after_action_re.html

Conatser, James L. & Vincent E. Grizio (December 2005). *Force XXI Battle Command Brigade and Below-Blue Force Tracking (FBCB2-BFT). A Case Study in the Accelerated Acquisition of a Digital Command and Control System during Operations Enduring Freedom and Iraqi Freedom.* MBA Thesis. Monterey, CA: Naval Postgraduate School.

Conroy, Capt Jason (2005). *Heavy Metal: A Tank Company's Battle to Baghdad.* Dulles, VA: Potomac Books.

Cordesman, Anthony (February 7, 2003). *Iraqi Armed Forces on the Edge of War.* Washington, DC: Center for Strategic and International Studies.

Cordesman, Anthony (July 21, 2003). *Lessons of the Iraq War: Main Report.* 11th working draft. Washington, DC: Center for Strategic and International Studies.

Department of the Army (August 2002). *Mechanized Infantry Platoon and Squad (Bradley)*, FM 3-21.71 (FM 7-7J). Washington, DC: Headquarters, Department of the Army.

Department of the Army (November 2003). *Bradley Gunnery*, FM-3-22.1 (FM 23-1). Washington, DC: Headquarters, Department of the Army.

DSCA (December 19, 2015). "Iraq—M1A1 Tanks." The Pentagon, VA: Defense Security Cooperation Agency: https://www.dsca.mil/press-media/major-arms-sales/iraq-m1a1-abrams-tanks

Edworthy, Niall (2010). *Main Battle Tank: The most dramatic account of British tank operations since WWII.* London: Penguin.

Gordon, John IV and Bruce R. Pirnie (2005). "'Everybody Wanted Tanks': Heavy Forces in Operation *Iraqi Freedom.*" *Joint Force Quarterly*, Issue 39, 4th Quarter, 2005.

Grummitt, David (2021). *Bradley Fighting Vehicle: The US Army's Combat-Proven Fighting Vehicle, 1981–2021.* Barnsley: Pen & Sword.

Haycraft, Travis (2018). *The Guns of al-Fao: Saddam, the War, and the Weapons that Made it Possible.* Undergraduate Honors Theses. Paper 1158. W&M ScholarWorks.

Holmes, Richard (2006). *Dusty Warriors: Modern Soldiers at War.* London: Harper Press.

Jean, Grace (October 1, 2005). "Stryker Units Win Over Skeptics." *National Defense*: https://www.nationaldefensemagazine.org/articles/2005/10/1/2005october--stryker-units-win-over-skeptics

McWilliams, Timothy S., with Nicholas J. Schlosser (2014). *US Marines in Battle: Fallujah November–December 2004.* Quantico, VA: US Marine Corps History Division.

Peters, Ralph (1997). "The Future of Armored Warfare." *Parameters*, 27, no. 3, 1997, doi:10.55540/0031-1723.1844.

Ripley, Tim (2016). *Operation Telic: The British Campaign in Iraq 2003–2009.* Lancaster: Telic-Herrick Publications.

Schulze, Carl (2006). *Iraq Insurgency: US Armored Vehicles in Action (Part 1).* Hong Kong: Concord Publications.

Spencer, John (January 31, 2019). "Stealing the Enemy's Urban Advantage: The Battle of Sadr City." Modern Warfare Institute, West Point: https://mwi.usma.edu/stealing-enemys-urban-advantage-battle-sadr-city/

Taylor, Dick (2018). *Owner's workshop Manual: Challenger 2 Main Battle Tank, 1998 to present.* Sparkford: Haynes Publishing.

Wood, Stephen (2015). *Those Terrible Grey Horses: An Illustrated History of the Royal Scots Dragoon Guards.* Oxford: Osprey Publishing.

Woods, K.M. (2006). *Iraqi Perspectives Project: a view of Operation Iraqi Freedom from Saddam's senior leadership.* Norfolk, VA: Joint Center for Operational Analysis.

INDEX

Note: page locators in bold refer to illustrations.